Coming Alive is about becoming fully engaged and energized in your chosen line of work. I can think of no one whose story (and advice) on this topic is more compelling or inspiring than Ruth Ross. Give yourself a present and your career a boost. Buy this book.
—Carol Kinsey Goman, Ph. D. Author of *The Silent Language of Leaders: How Body Language Can Help – or Hurt – How You Lead* and *The Truth About Lies in the Workplace: How to Spot Liars and What To Do About Them*

Coming Alive is a book that has broad appeal, on both a business and personal level. We all know someone that struggles with engagement, be it an associate, a colleague or a friend. With disengagement at an all time high, this is such a timely topic. Ruth has a wonderful combination of credibility and authenticity on this topic that comes across in her sage words. You will learn how to come alive which helps to create and maintain a "hugging culture".
—Jack Mitchell, Chairman, Mitchells Family of Stores. Author of *Hug Your Customers* and *Hug Your People*

Employee disengagement is the most destructive disease plaguing the business landscape today. Thankfully, *Coming Alive* has all the tools you need to cure it. This book is the best prescription for diagnosing and curing this epidemic and is a valuable resource for managers and employees alike.
—Jag Randhawa, Technology Executive and award-winning author of *The Bright Idea Box*

If we examine the current world of work, we will find that it is broken. There is an abundance of statistics and research studies telling us the extent of the crisis we face. What we don't have enough of are people like Ruth Ross who through her years of experience and wisdom have brought into the world a groundbreaking book on how to reengage our life and career. *Coming Alive* is a book I could not put down until I got to the end. It is full of insights, real life stories and actions that each of us can take to have a full life. I highly recommend it to anyone who wants to put their life and career on track.

—Ayelet Baron, Former Chief Strategy Officer, Cisco Canada, Futurist and Chief Instigator, Simplifying Work

This is such an important book! Ruth Ross treats this subject with great expertise and insight, while providing tangible, practical tools to identify, treat and turn disengagement around. She offers guidance from the perspective of both the manager and the employee that is clear and actionable. The stories she shares about real people will resonate with anyone who has been in the workplace. The assessment instruments she created and her simple process for preventing disengagement in the workplace are powerful tools for an effective leader to use.

—Cheryl Ellis, Trusted business advisor and high performance coach, Founder, Ellis Business Enterprises, LLC.

This insightful book, written by someone with firsthand knowledge of the subject matter is a must read for anyone who has a job or is looking for one. Ruth Ross shares both her personal experience and business expertise about one of the biggest challenges facing organizations today; the proliferation of disengagement at work and at home. Ross proves to us in her book that it is possible to reengage and cure the disengagement disease.

—Dana Manciagli, Author of *Cut The Crap, Get A JOB! A New Job Search Process for a New Era*

In *Coming Alive*, Ruth Ross addresses the silent killer of organizations, employee disengagement, and offers ways to reignite passion and commitment for employees, managers, and beyond. She acutely points out the connection of engagement between personal and professional lives and how to take the matter into your own hands. Ruth's non-apologetic approach in highlighting the systemic failures and her unwavering desire to help organizations breakdown the issue is admirable.

—Hsiang-Yi Lin, CEO of MKMB Coaching and Consulting, Author of *A Practical Guide to Authentic Leadership: A 60-Day Journey that Unlocks the True Leader in You*

Ruth Ross writes about this topic with the passion and clarity of someone who has gone on her own journey to reengage, both personally and professionally. Scattered through the book are stories of others whose lives have also been touched by disengagement, along with easy-to-use strategies, tips, and tools for reengagement. Anyone who runs a business today needs to read this book.

—Wilkes Bashford, Founder of Wilkes Bashford Stores

COMING ALIVE

The Journey to Reengage
Your Life and Career

Elizabeth,

Enjoy The Journey!

Ruth

RUTH K. ROSS

Coming Alive: The Journey to Reengage Your Life and Career
By Ruth Ross
1. SEL 000000 Self Help - General 2. BUS 012000 Business - Careers/General 3. BUS 041000 Business - Management

ISBN: 978-1-935953-64-7

Cover design by Lewis Agrell

Printed in the United States of America

Authority Publishing
11230 Gold Express Dr. #310-413
Gold River, CA 95670
800-877-1097
www.AuthorityPublishing.com

Contents

Acknowledgements

A huge thank you to the following special people:

The most important person in my life, my amazing and loving husband Sandy who always believes in me and supports whatever I do. He knew I had it in me to write this book long before I believed it myself.

My parents, Anne and Ed Kamens who always instilled in their daughters a drive to succeed in whatever we chose to do and to never forget that you need to be passionate about what you do.

My sister and bother-in-law Gilbey and Brian Campbell for taking on so much of the family responsibility with grace and dignity and always encouraging me to follow my dreams. You are simply the best people, period.

Greg Benzon, my best friend, former work spouse and partner in crime. You were the one who first put the spark in me to write (although we were supposed to do it together…) and now it's your turn.

John, Caroline, Christine and Barry, the other members of the Six Pack who are so dear to us. We've shared countless laughs and memories together and so many more to come. I appreciate your support and encouragement and willingness to celebrate all the milestones along the way.

Stephanie and Sue at Authority Publishing, thank you for having faith in my book and working so seamlessly with me to bring it to life.

Finally, I want to send a special thank you to Justin Spizman for his help in the creation of this book. It was 'bashert' that we met and for that I am forever grateful. Your skills far transcend the writing process. You have this unbelievable way of connecting with your clients and their written words to help fashion the best book possible. There is no way Coming Alive would have been completed without your help.

Chapter One

THE EXCITEMENT OF ENGAGEMENT IN LIFE AND IN WORK

*M*ost times, when we hear the word *engagement* we immediately travel to that exciting moment when two people come together and pledge love, dedication, and the remainder of their lives to one another. It is that special moment when two become one and where lives intersect and eventually merge into one another. Engagement is a special and meaningful moment, celebrated by all and filled with undeniable hope, happiness, and excitement. In the movie *When Harry Met Sally*, title character Harry says, "When you realize you want to spend the rest of your life with somebody, you want the rest of your life to start as soon as possible." We all desire the activation of that special moment when it all comes together, feels right, and makes perfect sense.

But engagement is more than the magical moment that occurs between two people. Engagement is the act of pledging yourself and dedicating your life not just to a person, but also to a mission, vision, or purpose. Engagement can be between two people or it can occur at an exquisite level between your heart and soul and career. We all desire to feel highly connected with what we do.

Consider these examples:

Engagement is when a doctor passionately tells you he doesn't practice medicine, he saves lives.

Engagement is when an attorney indicates he doesn't practice personal injury law, but that he stands up for people who can no longer stand on their own.

Engagement is when a restaurant owner tells you he started his business to honor his family's tradition and makes his own pasta from scratch every morning because "that's the way Nana taught me to make it."

Engagement is when the manager at a mom-and-pop pharmacy opens the doors an hour after closing because a customer needs medicine for his sick child.

Engagement is what motivates people not only to feel dedicated to their job and their life, but also to feel rewarded by what they do and how they do it. It pushes people to look at things differently and go above and beyond, not because they have to but because they *want* to. Engagement is buying in, going all in, and remaining within and contributing to the passion and mission of the company. It is what separates the striving companies from the thriving companies, the happy folks from the unhappy ones, the smiles from the frowns, and the success stories from the shattered dreams.

We all want to be engaged. We all want to avoid disengagement. That is the easy part to declare. But the "how" is not so easy. And together that is where our story begins. Our journey through engagement starts with a humble shoe company based out of Las Vegas.

So many companies around the world get it "right" when it comes to engagement. Throughout this book we will highlight some that stand out since we all know that imitation is the sincerest form of flattery. We can all learn from others who truly focus on engaging their employees at an unbelievably high level.

THE RIGHT FORMULA FOR WOW

The last thing you'd envision is a company where the CEO offers to pay you to leave. That is, pays you to leave in the interest of creating a fully engaged workforce of committed and passionate people furthering the mission of the organization. And that's exactly what is happening at Zappos, the company that is always top-of-mind when we think about organizations that strive for high employee engagement.

The visionaries behind Zappos always knew they wanted to create a different kind of environment within their company. It wasn't just about filling a void in the retail world or even selling shoes online. Rather, their goal was to create a WOW experience not just for their customers but also for their employees. From the beginning, the company's CEO, Tony Hsieh, focused on building a workplace that aligned its employees with the company's core values. Putting those two together, he knew they could accomplish amazing things.

At Zappos, it all starts with hiring people who look beyond the basics of a job description and who can visualize themselves "living" the company's ten core values. Since candidates are put through a rigorous screening process, it's not easy to get hired by Zappos. Once someone applies for a job, it involves a three-stage process.

The first step is a recruiting phone screen, conducted by a company recruiter to determine if the applicant's core values match those of the organization and to ensure there are no deal breakers, like an unwillingness to relocate to their headquarters.

The next step in the recruiting process is a phone interview to assess the candidate's technical fit for the job. When a candidate completes the first two screens, it's on to the final onsite portion of the selection process, which is much more than just a face-to-face interview. The meeting includes additional assessment tests and technical interviews, this time with other members of the prospective team. A key component of the day is the tour of the offices, where the prospective employee gets a chance to see what it's like to work at Zappos. At the same time, the host is able to judge the candidate's unvarnished reaction and determine their level of interest and excitement.

The day concludes with a core-value interview to ensure the candidate understands the unique culture of Zappos. Understandably, it's quite a process. But as shown in numerous studies by firms such as The Gallup Organization, Towers Perrin, and McKinsey, a significant correlation exists between an effective hiring process and high engagement levels in the workplace.

If this company pays so much attention on the front end to selecting the right team, then why pay someone to leave? It seems counterintuitive, doesn't it? All of Zappos' new employees go through an intensive one-month on-boarding process. During this training period, which includes a full immersion into their unique corporate culture, employees determine if Zappos is the right fit for them. It's a two-way street. If new employees are not 100 percent sure they can support the mission and vision of Zappos, they have an out. In fact, Zappos is even willing to pay for the work already completed and throw in an additional $3,000 check for the former employee's honesty and candid behavior. No questions asked, no back and forth—they just get to take the money and run.

Why would a company offer to pay someone to leave after only a few weeks on the job? You'd think they would be afraid potential employees would line up just to get the money. But internal audits show that only 3 percent of new employees actually take Zappos up on the offer. That's a testament to a great recruiting process designed to filter out and hire only the employees committed to building a career at Zappos. It's a small cost to incur compared to what it would take to fill a slew of open positions or to replace trained but disengaged employees.

Zappos is known for having a culture that embraces and encourages fun, but that doesn't mean employees don't take the work seriously. The passion they have for providing a "wow" experience for their customers is legendary. At Zappos, each team member recognizes he has a stake in the success or failure of the company and is aligned around the business's core vision and values. Zappos is a great example of a company that has successfully bridged the gap between engaged employees and engaged customers by building a belief in the brand promise.

This is a company that truly understands how to create the perfect engagement cocktail: three parts hard work, two parts commitment, one part focus, and one part fun. Throw it all in the blender and mix it up. What comes pouring out is a "wow" experience for all involved.

CONNECTING THE DOTS

Consider the last time you were fully connected, linked, and dedicated to something with every ounce of your heart and soul. Not to a brand-new car or beautiful home, or any of the material items you have acquired. Let's dive deeper and focus on the last opportunity you had to honestly look at your professional life and feel a sense of fulfillment, maybe even true happiness. Think about the love you have for your friends and family members, or maybe even for a hobby or other rewarding endeavor. The time you spend with these people and participating in these moments feels hearty and satisfying, doesn't it?

You probably feel fully engaged, have little desire to be elsewhere, and walk away feeling refreshed and warm inside, right? This sense of nourishment, prosperity, and rejuvenation is food for the soul; it creates and preserves joy.

But what about the times you aren't lost in those moments? Do you feel the same way? Do you even feel fulfilled? The average American spends almost two-thirds of his life working. He will have logged over 84,560 hours at his job by the time he is at the age of retirement. Take a moment to look at your daily routine. It probably consists of waking up, having a quick bite, then heading to your job. You remain there for most of your waking hours and then head back home to spend time with your family.

Are you happy with your current career? Do you even consider it to be a career? The notion of engagement is an exciting one, and feeling fulfilled at work is an enormous accomplishment. It is rewarding and positively impacts every facet of your life. Now think about the occasions you left work unhappy. Did it impact your personal life? Finding yourself stuck in an unfulfilling career is a debilitating reality. Wondering if there is a way out is unbelievably depressing. You don't have to be unhappy and unfulfilled with your professional or personal life. There is a better way. Happiness and fulfillment are yours for the taking if you simply recognize the lack thereof and are willing to address it.

Your work life is like a journey without a roadmap or GPS system. You begin with a basic understanding of where you want to go and how you plan to get there. Unlike a road trip to a specific destination, however, with this journey you can't simply plug in an address and have a soothing voice guide you to your ultimate goal. During your career you will take many twists and turns, all in the search of the Holy Grail we call passion, fulfillment, and engagement. At times we all take wrong turns, but it's how you readjust and move forward that make the difference.

This book will take you on a journey through engagement, navigating a detour into disengagement, and ending at the ultimate destination of personal and professional reengagement.

YOU CAN'T SPELL TEAM WITHOUT THE "E" OF ENGAGEMENT

Engagement is not one-dimensional and it doesn't discriminate. It happens in all facets of life, from school to sports to friendships to relationships and everything in between. It can be effortless and natural when done well. It can result in big successes, such as winning a World Series or creating a healthy marriage. The same holds true for building engagement in the workplace. Employees want nothing more than to be part of something meaningful and feel like they've had a hand in making a difference. They want to be part of something bigger than themselves and part of the underlying success. They want to be energized by their job and look forward to going to work, willing to put in the extra effort it takes to make their organization a success.

The truth is it's really hard to win a championship in any team sport without alignment around a shared goal. In the first round of the 2012 Major League Baseball playoffs, my hometown San Francisco Giants baseball team found themselves down two games to none and facing elimination in a "best of five" series. Outfielder Hunter Pence was the inspirational leader of the club and nicknamed "The Reverend" by his teammates. Before this crucial game, he stood up in the locker room and questioned the commitment and engagement of his teammates. He loudly proclaimed that he wanted to be there and was not ready to go home. He questioned the passion of his fellow players. Of course he used more colorful language, but you get the point. They all joined Hunter in proclaiming that they wanted to win it all. They went out and won the next three games in a row to defeat the Cincinnati Reds.

Next up was a seven-game series with the St. Louis Cardinals. Three games later the Giants found themselves down three games to none and once again facing elimination. But they had been here before. "The Reverend" got up once more and begged his teammates to work together to reach their goal of winning the division series. In yet another historic rally, they came back to win four straight games and reach the World Series. This was baseball history; no other Major League team had ever come back this way in two consecutive series.

It was once again Hunter's stage before game one of the World Series. However, he knew that comebacks weren't going to be necessary this time as he stood up in front of his teammates before another critical game. He knew he was looking at a highly engaged, committed team. The Giants went on to sweep the Detroit Tigers in four straight games to win their second world championship in just three years.

The Giants would not have cemented their place in Major League Baseball history if everyone on the team was not focused on the end goal and 100 percent engaged in the quest. It's hard to stay fully engaged through a 162-game season; performance ebbs and flows based on unplanned-for circumstances like player injuries and the overall cohesiveness of the team. It wasn't just up to the coach to lead the team. Rather, engagement had to involve everyone from the equipment manager to the trainer to each and every member of the team. That's no different from any other kind of workplace team; it's all about everyone coming together with one goal in mind. There's no "I" in team for a reason.

WHY DOES ENGAGEMENT MATTER?

Employee engagement isn't just another concept invented to keep human resources professionals employed and corporate leaders ready to put in their earplugs. There is a clear connection and definite ROI (return on investment) when companies focus on creating an engaged and committed workplace. Especially over the last five years, statistics abound that demonstrate the economic value of a highly engaged workforce. It's not a stretch to say that companies with high disengagement can ultimately find themselves out of business if they don't reengage team members. In fact, according to The Gallup Organization, the cost of lost productivity in the US alone due to disengagement is $500 billion per year.

Research proves that engaged employees are more productive and focused on quality, resulting in higher customer satisfaction and higher profits. The Corporate Leadership Council studied the engagement level of employees around the world. They found that engaged companies increase profits as much as three times faster than their competitors who are not engaged. In their 2012 study, engagement researchers McLean & Company found that organizations with highly engaged employees had an average three-year revenue growth of 20.1 percent versus 8.9 percent for companies with average to low engagement.

The most successful senior leaders understand the ROI of engagement and recognize that it will be next to impossible to achieve their goals without a fully committed and engaged workforce. Employee engagement is a top business priority for them, particularly in today's tough business climate. They know that having a high-performing workforce is essential for growth and survival. They treat employees as valuable people with skills rather than people with valuable skills.

Dick Kovacevich, the former chairman and CEO of Wells Fargo, authored the vision and values for his company that are still being followed today, including his prophetic statement that "People Are Our Competitive Advantage." Dick liked to say that he wouldn't be worried if he left his company playbook on an airplane because although his competitors offered the same products and services, the differentiator was how his company executed that plan. It is always about the people. He recognized that highly engaged workforces could increase innovation, productivity, and bottom-line performance while simultaneously reducing costs related to hiring and retention in increasingly competitive talent markets.

Be it a corporate CEO, a coach of a sports team, a director of a play, or a pastor of a church, all leaders need to understand what the return on investment of engagement will bring to them. Creating an environment where engagement is fostered and supported will manifest many benefits in the long run as evidenced by lower turnover, higher employee satisfaction, and increased profitability.

AN ENGAGING HISTORY LESSON

Employee engagement isn't a new concept; it's been around since the 1920s. However, in 1990 the focus of engagement switched to assessing job satisfaction and organization commitment. In the early 2000s, many companies jumped on the bandwagon and started surveying their employees, first focusing on satisfaction, then honing in on engagement.

In June 2013, The Gallup Organization released the results of their updated Workplace Survey focused on employee engagement—and heads turned. To stunned readers, the survey revealed that only 30 percent of US workers identified themselves as engaged at work. What about the other 70 percent? That's the percentage of the workforce that said they felt disengaged, with 18 percent of these employees identified as actively disengaged. Engagement quickly became a trending topic on both traditional and social media. The results of the survey were discussed on *The Today Show, Live with Kelly and Michael, NBC Nightly News,* and *The David Letterman Show.* They even appeared in popular leadership blogs like Forbes. com and *The Huffington Post.*

Overnight, the word *disengagement* became one of the most talked-about terms, not just as it related to the workplace but also to life in general. It forced people to look deep inside to see if they were one of the 70 percent, and when the shift from engagement to disengagement even occurred. Most disengaged workers can describe "the moment" they lost touch. They know if it came at the end of a long workday or in the middle of a sleepless night. They know if it struck during the droning on of a conference call or in a quiet moment of reflection. They know if it came out of the blue or was just the straw that broke the camel's back. They can tell you what work they were doing and, with absolute clarity, when and why they stopped caring about it.

The world is full of moments when people cross the line from engagement into disengagement, replacing creativity and passion with stagnation and resentment. This happens with much greater frequency in the workplace, but it isn't just a nine-to-five affliction. It can happen to anyone regardless of ethnicity, gender, age, marital status, geography, or job title. Disengagement doesn't discriminate—and it truly is a global affair.

Is engagement just another in a long line of HR buzzwords, or is it something that is important to understand? Is it a phenomenon specific to the workplace or to life in general? The answer to all four questions is yes.

DEFINING ENGAGEMENT

The most often-used definition is that employee engagement is a measure of an employee's positive or negative emotional attachment to their job, colleagues, and organization that profoundly influences their willingness to learn and perform at work. From a personal perspective, engagement is the measure of a person's involvement in social, leisure, and productive activities and how that correlates to happiness and wellbeing.

There are three distinct categories of engagement and corresponding behavioral traits:

HIGHLY ENGAGED

Highly engaged workers begin with the goal in mind, know exactly what's expected of them, and work to achieve it. They proactively seek out opportunities for growth and ways to excel. They look for opportunities to provide input to decisions that affect their organization. Engaged employees spend time building relationships and strive to create a positive work environment. They produce more in less time, contribute to the bottom line, are loyal, and stay with their company longer.

DISENGAGED

Disengaged employees come to work and concentrate on the tasks at hand, but not on outcomes. They have no desire to provide input and just want to be told what to do, get paid, and then go home. Sometimes they are referred to as "fence-sitters" who could turn around with some care and feeding or slide further into disengagement. They get little satisfaction out of their work and are not loyal to the organization.

ACTIVELY DISENGAGED

Actively disengaged workers psychologically cut their ties to the organization; they express mistrust and show their animosity to others. They are very vocal in their feelings and damage their organization's reputation. These employees are both resistant to change and quick to find fault. Unlike the "fence-sitters," these people are very difficult to turn around and in all likelihood have burned too many bridges to ever be successful at their current job.

Leading an organization comprised solely of engaged employees is essentially a pipe dream in today's workplace. However, that doesn't mean you can't strive for a higher percentage of engaged workers than your competitors.

Feeling valued, being confident in what you do, remaining inspired by your company's mission, being empowered to make a difference and enthusiastic for what lies ahead are all key emotions that lead to engagement. Employees want and even need to be part of something bigger than them—something of which they can be proud. Engaged employees look forward to going to work and are more willing to put in extra effort to make the organization a success. Engagement is clearly demonstrated by how personally connected and committed workers feel to their organization.

Based on a number of different factors, people will naturally slide back and forth between engagement and disengagement during their working lives. It's like being on a seesaw where at any given moment you could be all the way up on top, bumping the ground, or balanced right in the middle. Where you ultimately land can be due to an action on your part or because of something outside your control. Getting comfortable with riding the seesaw and knowing what it takes to achieve balance is what it's all about.

THE MAGIC OF ENGAGEMENT

How do you as a leader solve the engagement puzzle? It starts with ensuring that goal alignment is well communicated and occurring at every level of the organization. Top managers should be expected to set and communicate business objectives. Middle managers are responsible for creating specific objectives for their employees that support those broader business goals. Finally, all employees need some level of autonomy and accountability for meeting their individual goals.

It also starts with understanding the key elements to engagement. Here are some of the most important ones:

- *Create a clear set of company values that are known and understood by everyone, regardless of their job title.*

- *Ensure your employees are aligned with the company's vision, values, mission, and goals.*

- *Build culture intentionally by focusing on those things that support the kind of organization you aspire to lead.*

- *Select and train the right managers. All too often companies tap someone on the shoulder because they've been a great individual contributor and say, "Congratulations, you are now a manager."*

- *Enable people's success by ensuring they have the tools, resources, and support needed to do their jobs effectively.*

Culture and engagement go hand in hand. It's hard to separate them. If you have a strong corporate culture, it's likely that you have a higher level of engagement. But even having reached corporate culture nirvana doesn't mean it will stay there. Numerous factors can trouble the foundation, such as needing to make a tough business decision like entering into a merger or implementing cost reductions or cutting a key member of a team that isn't performing. One key is how the negative messages are given and received.

SIX C'S OF ENGAGEMENT

As a general rule of thumb, amazing businesses succeed in creating engaged organizations by focusing on these six C's:

Collaboration: Employees don't just work together; they are vested in each other's success. Collaborative organizations know there is more power in "we" than in "I."

Creativity: Employees are heard and their ideas are valued. Engaged employees are more likely to be innovative and creative.

Connection: Engaged employees create engaged customers who create more sales. There's no denying the cause and effect of this relationship.

Celebration: You celebrate your successes along the way so that employees can feel a sense of accomplishment and recognition. There's nothing better than having a reason to celebrate.

Community: You forge the connection between your employees and the communities in which they live and work by giving back. Here's where your work and personal life can come together in brilliant harmony.

IT'S ALL IN THE CONTEXT

Saving the most important "C" for last, let's talk about the one thing that can make or break a company's ability to create a workforce full of engaged employees. That "C" stands for **Context**. The simple act of providing context for decisions is the most powerful thing a leader can do to foster the right environment. Nothing rips at the fabric of trust more than not knowing or understanding why a decision was made. It's okay to share bad news, but at least let your employees understand the reason behind it. If you have to announce layoffs, explain the business reason driving that decision. If you are granting employees something positive, like a performance-related bonus, give them the facts behind the decision so they can see how their hard work is paying off with strong results for the company.

If you remember nothing but this one thing after reading this book, never forget to give people context. It works in your life outside of work as well. No matter the situation, everyone wants to know the *why* behind the *what*. Context helps to provide clarity, direction, and meaning and serves to get everyone aligned on the same page. If you ask parents how many times they've heard their children respond "Why?" to a request, the answer will probably be: "Too many times to count." But if you provide the context beforehand you might be able to lessen the number of whys down the road and head off that migraine headache before it starts.

VISION QUEST AND THE SECRET SAUCE

The following is an example of how all the C's came together in an engaging manner for a top organization. The company that got it right in the late '90s was Charles Schwab, the brokerage firm headquartered in San Francisco. I was fortunate to have worked for them from 1996–2002 during their high-growth days and then on through the dot-com bust that impacted not just startups but many other companies as well.

Back then Schwab had a very strong corporate culture that provided an environment where people could thrive and achieve professional success. In the late '90s, Schwab reached a high of number five on the *Fortune* list of Top Companies to Work For. This was mostly the result of their focus on creating an environment based on a strong corporate culture and that fostered high employee engagement.

Schwab figured out that the secret sauce of engagement was communication, context, and alignment. This meant ensuring that their employees were all on the same page when it came to the company's mission and strategic priorities. In 1999 a small group of us were incredibly lucky to be asked to work on an experience called Vision Quest.

Vision Quest was a project based on a fairly new concept called a *learning map*. We partnered with an outside consulting firm called Root Learning, which designed a large picture map that colorfully highlighted the firm's vision, mission, values, strategic priorities, and competitive landscape. This learning map was then turned into a game designed to teach our employees about the company and its challenges, ending with everyone fully aware of and aligned with the go-forward company strategy.

On a Saturday, a non-work day for the majority of the organization, all fourteen thousand employees gathered in thirteen locations including overseas, all satellite linked-in to the San Francisco site. We sat at tables of ten that were mixed in terms of levels and job functions, with a full-sized replica of the learning map as the game board in front of us.

The day started with a passionate welcome by both the chairman and the CEO, which provided context for why we were all there on a weekend and the importance of the task ahead of us. Shortly thereafter, the bell rang and the competition was on. Once the game was underway, the grumblings and mutterings about working on a Saturday gave way to passion and excitement about the journey ahead. Soon it wasn't about who would win the game but rather about the challenges that faced us. Ideas started flowing like water. As the buzz in the room got louder and louder, this went on for a few hours and ended in a crescendo of excitement to come in on Monday and get started on the next set of challenges. The day culminated with a cake-and-champagne celebration honoring the company's twenty-fifth anniversary.

Vision Quest was a watershed moment for Schwab. Employees from all over the company were heard saying: "Now I get where we're going and how I fit in." The employee survey conducted later that year showed a major up-tick in engagement and satisfaction as the aftereffects of this alignment exercise still reverberated throughout the organization.

YOU CAN'T COMPARTMENTALIZE YOUR LIFE

No matter how engaged and happy you are in the workplace, or conversely how disengaged and unhappy you are, it will inevitably impact your life outside of work. If you are unhappy in your personal life for any number of reasons, it's hard to leave that at the door when you walk into your office. On the flipside, if you are being bullied at work, frustrated by a lack of appreciation or recognition, or simply in the wrong job, do you really believe those things won't follow you home and affect your personal life? Either way, you will find yourself disengaged in some segment of your life.

When it comes to engagement, most people are not even aware of the connection between their work and personal life outside the office. We all tend to compartmentalize ourselves to make it easier to cope. It's easier to focus on work when at the office and your personal life when at home. Where things get difficult is at the intersection of your personal and professional life. For example, if you are dealing with a major life stress such as a marriage breaking up, can you really turn that off when in the workplace?

Normally highly engaged and passionate about his work, one of my colleagues spent months quietly shutting himself in his office, barely smiling and appearing completely disconnected from his coworkers. Out of respect, I gave him the space to deal with whatever was bothering him, hoping that at some point he'd confide in me. Eventually others in the department also noticed the change in his behavior and began chatting about it.

Just as I was getting ready to ask him if everything was okay, he told me that his marriage was falling apart. All I could do was offer a supportive ear and let him know I was there for him. The act of discussing his personal life was therapeutic and the key to his personal reengagement. I didn't have to do a thing other than listen when warranted. The burden of the secret caused his workplace disengagement, and once that obstacle was removed he was able to turn his energy and focus back on the work.

On the other hand, how many of us can truly leave the stresses of work behind when we go home? If your boss is yelling at you, are you more inclined to go home and yell at someone else? Probably so. It happens more than people would like to admit. If you are frustrated by a lack of appreciation for all your hard work and feel like you are invisible—even in a very visible position—does that feeling just go away the minute you walk into your home? Probably not.

Many people self-medicate with drugs or alcohol to numb the pain incurred during the workday. Millions are suffering with depression and carry that with them throughout the workday and then to their home. You can't just flip a switch when you go to work, leaving your stressors at home. Conversely, you can't stuff your problems in a file drawer at your office as you leave for the day. We are who we are, no matter where we are.

CAN YOU REALLY GO OUT OF BUSINESS DUE TO DISENGAGEMENT?

Each and every day some company around the globe goes out of business, partly because they lost their way and ended up with a disengaged workforce. It's not very often that an organization can pull itself out of a tailspin and come back from the brink, but it absolutely can happen.

Stories abound of companies that get it right as it relates to engagement and its connection to business success. Unfortunately, many more just flat-out don't get it and are hanging on by a thread. The key is to understand that engagement is a person-by-person task. If even one person is not engaged—particularly if that person is a manager—then you can't have a fully energized workforce. Think of it as lights on a Christmas tree. If one bulb goes out, the rest can't shimmer as brightly. The key is to understand what causes the lights to dim inside of people.

Now that you've got the context for the journey to reengagement, pack your bags and let's get started!

Chapter Two

THE DISSECTION OF DISENGAGEMENT

*A*ccording to the Collins dictionary, "Disengagement is a process by which people gradually stop being involved in a conflict, activity or organization."

To many people, disengagement can feel like a series of small paper cuts, while to others it feels more like getting hit by an oncoming bus. The initial impact is a searing pain. The side effects can linger for a very long time. Disengagement is personal in nature and affects each person individually. Like a snowflake, no two stories are ever alike. But all disengagement can have a monumental impact on life. Every disengaged person has a reason for why they transformed into an unhappy and dissatisfied worker. And everyone deals with that feeling differently. The one constant: there is always some underlying cause or trigger for the disengagement. There is always that "moment."

THE TREE OF LIFE

All new trees begin with just a seed. Once a tree is planted, roots grow underground and spread. The naked eye can't perceive the vast and growing roots; we can only focus on the tree trunk, branches, or leaves. What's invisible to us from ground level is how the tree has manifested underground and whether an ailment is stunting its growth. If there is a disease impacting its roots, we won't know that until something else happens to help surface the problem. Before the tree can be treated, and hopefully saved, we need to know the exact cause of the problem.

Disengagement is a lot like a sick tree. On the surface our physical attributes might show a happy, satisfied person, but underneath, at our roots—those things which support us and keep us steady and strong—something is dreadfully wrong, spreading discontent and malaise throughout our whole being. In order to heal, we must first identify the underlying cause.

It's pretty common to see a disengaged person smile on the outside while feeling enormous pain on the inside. We've all become masters of disguise, whether at work or with our loved ones. We've become conditioned to the cycle, and it can be a great coping mechanism. The problem is, like our tree of life, one day it will shed its leaves, lose its color and vibrancy, and eventually die. Unfortunately, we can't hide behind the smile forever.

THE WORKPLACE IS A BREEDING GROUND OF DISENGAGEMENT

Disengagement doesn't just show up one day on a whim. Usually one or more gradual factors have a bearing on this issue and cause it to rear its ugly head. Disengagement is not a sudden experience. It occurs over a period of time and slowly eats away at the passion you have for your job until there is none left. Many of the causes of disengagement are linked together, but you don't need to experience all of them to become a target of the disengagement disease—even one can cause your roots to rot.

There are five main reasons (and a number of other small, related ones) that drive disengagement. Taken alone, each of these has a significant impact on the level of engagement a person can have in their job. Think about what could happen if more than one of these were tied together. Remember, disengagement is a *choice*. It may not feel like it in the moment, but we all have the opportunity to fight back or simply give in to whatever ails us. However, the first step in curing disengagement is to recognize and acknowledge the issue.

In this chapter we will profile five employees to illustrate each of the underlying causes of disengagement. This should help you begin your journey of self-discovery and ultimately arrive in the reengagement phase of the trip.

DISENGAGED EMPLOYEE #1: HEY, THIS JOB ISN'T WHAT YOU PROMISED ME

Sally is an eager, motivated young professional who has worked in a series of customer-facing jobs since graduating college two years ago. She's always been told that she is great with people and believed that the right career direction for her was to get hired by a stable, profitable company in the financial services industry that was known for outstanding customer service. Imagine her excitement when Acme Bank, one of the top financial services organizations in the Midwest, hired her to work in their customer call center.

Sally's job was to answer calls from clients with questions about their retail banking accounts and to help solve any issues they may have. On her first day, she arrived at a cubicle with a computer, a phone, a headset, and a thick manual full of procedures and processes. At the time, she didn't have a clue as to what came next. No one was assigned to her as a mentor, no supervisor came by to welcome her, and no one offered her any guidance. She was expected to pick up the phone when it rang. This went on day after day, and Sally eventually became more adept at her job and comfortable with the required service-level standards.

But she never felt happy or committed to her job.

How many of us have experienced an interview process (sometimes a lengthy, exhausting one) that sold a pretty picture of what the job entailed, only to find out later it was an entirely different experience? This happens all the time. It isn't unusual to be misled about the job responsibilities or even the job itself.

It is unrealistic to think a job description will always be an exact mirror of the job in action, but it's also not unreasonable to expect that the job *resemble* the description during the interview process. When that doesn't turn out to be the case, it can lead to feelings of frustration or even betrayal by the hired employee. These are roads that can lead straight into disengagement. No matter how well a job is described, sometimes if it's a new experience, no amount of initial explanation can truly represent the actuality of the role.

Call centers are the poster child for this kind of reality show. Even if the interviewer was incredibly detailed in how he described the job, if you have never worked in that particular environment, you have no idea what it's like to answer calls all day from unhappy customers while under tight productivity measures. The result can be a quick and steady downward slope of emotions and resentment toward the job. You begin to question your decision, feel as if you were taken advantage of, and eventually disengage.

THE RIGHT FOOT

Regardless of function, level, or industry, no job is immune to this notion of the position not matching what was promised. It's all part of starting off on the right foot with honest employers who are realistic and respectful. The result will be a more loyal, connected, and excited team willing to contribute at a maximum level if they are clear on the expectations set forth for them from day one.

This isn't just a basic tenet for someone new to a role. As priorities shift and other things come into play, jobs can and will change over time. It is incumbent on the manager and employee to meet periodically to reset expectations and goals.

The smartest leaders are those who understand that engagement really starts during the hiring process. That meeting is the first opportunity to build trust and demonstrate to your potential hire that you care about him and his engagement with the job. I recently had a conversation with Don Fornes, founder and CEO of Software Advice, about employee engagement. Don has done a phenomenal job of creating an engaged workforce. I inquired about his secret sauce. Here's one of the keys to success he shared with me:

"I tell my managers to get the right people in the right seats. It all starts with hiring and then giving our people autonomy. We give each person their own project, which is special and apart from their regular job. I want them to own it. I show people early on what the path for them looks like. I tell them: while you may be doing this job today, a year from now you will be doing this other job and make this amount of money. I believe everyone needs a vision."

When a job doesn't match the expectations and leadership takes no action to remedy the situation, employees will likely just go through the motions without any commitment or loyalty to their employer, all the while having their frustration build.

THE CURE

It all starts with an effective recruiting process. Companies need to be more committed to taking their time and getting it right. We're not just talking about putting "butts in chairs." In the spirit of Zappos, recruiting should be a multistage process. Here are some key steps to consider for your hiring process:

- Create a thorough job description that details all the major tasks expected of the employee. Included in the description should be a list of any measurements or standards for this role (i.e., production numbers, sales quotas, etc.), so there is no confusion as to what is required of the employee.

- Give a copy of the description to anyone interviewing for the role so you are both on the same page.

- Thoroughly pre-screen all applicants to make sure they meet the basic requirements for the job before moving to the next phase of the interview process.

- Using the job description, create a series of behavioral-based interview questions designed to elicit examples of how the candidate has handled these kinds of situations before. The best predictor of future behavior is past performance.

- Select a team of interviewers that can each hone in on different things. For example, one person might be focused on questions regarding customer service skills, another on how someone approaches teamwork with colleagues, and a third on how they manage others.

- Offer prospective candidates a chance to look around the workplace to get a sense of what the environment will be like.

- Make sure that throughout the entire process your candidates feel comfortable asking questions and clarifying what they've heard so far. Those who don't ask any questions usually haven't done their homework, which is a big red flag.

- Look for people who talk about what they can do for the company versus what the company can do for them. It will increase your odds of hiring someone predisposed to commitment and engagement.

DISENGAGED EMPLOYEE #2: IS THIS ALL THERE IS?

Robin is really good at her job; she should be after doing it for more than ten years. As the finance manager for the operations division at Smith Brothers manufacturing, Robin started out doing planning and analysis of the division's financial results before earning a promotion to the next level within two years of joining the team.

While there, she supervised a team of eight and reported directly to the head of operations. Over the eight years that Robin's been in her current position, nothing much has changed in terms of her job description. Even though she's always gotten high performance ratings and is continuously told she has high potential, no additional duties have been given to her. Over time she experienced turnover on her team when her staff felt frustrated that they were not growing and able to move into an expanded role. Every time Robin applied for a new job within the company, her boss either talked her out of it or told the new hiring manager that he couldn't let her go at that point in time.

She eventually went to her boss's manager to talk about this and inquire why she was blocked from moving; she was told that she was really needed in her current role. To make matters even worse, her salary was frozen due to company policy, making her ineligible for any merit increase. No wonder why Robin eventually disengaged in this role.

The notion of a career ladder where you work hard to move up one rung at a time is long gone in today's workplace. However, people still strive for something more. Today's concept of career development is much more of an abstract pattern where you can move up, down, or sideways as you add new skills to your portfolio. It's all about learning and new experiences—in the hope that this will eventually lead you to a different opportunity and potentially more money. The key is not to be complacent and idle in one place.

For too many people, the journey has dead-ended and there is no more movement in their current roles. When that happens, employees feel stuck in their jobs, with no identified pathway out. When people work at the same jobs for extended time periods, they can also be subjected to a freeze in their compensation because they are at the maximum cap of their company's salary structure. Resentment will eventually set in.

If this occurs, it's not uncommon to see an employee lose their passion for their job and to feel that there's no reason to put forth maximum effort for what seems like little to no reward. In addition, the employee feels that he has no out and needs to hold onto his job instead of finding a new job and exiting the workplace. It doesn't have to be this way.

THE CURE

It all needs to start with a conversation. Managers and employees should establish an open dialogue about how things are going on the job. One can't simply assume that his manager is a mind reader who knows—but chooses to ignore—that employees feel stuck in their jobs. Likewise, managers can't take silence as a sign of contentment and engagement. Here are some things employees can do to get unstuck and managers should do to reignite their employees.

- Employees who feel stuck in their current roles and don't see a way out need to do their homework to explore what new opportunities might be out there. They can't wait for a tap on the shoulder that may never occur.

- If you work for a company that has an internal job-posting system, USE IT! The purpose of a companywide job-posting process is to facilitate movement internally. There are usually policies in place to support you transferring without fear of reprisal from your current manager.

- Identify people in other areas that interest you. Seek them out for an informational interview. This process will assist you in understanding where your skills might be transferable and help you to build your network in the event that something may open up down the road.

- Look deep inside yourself to pinpoint what's keeping you stuck in the same place. If it's something fixable then speak up. You can't expect someone to know what's bothering you if you don't talk about it.

- Set up a meeting to talk with your boss about your career. Don't make it confrontational. Rather, talk about how you are feeling and how it's impacting your job. Ask what it will take to move to the next level or learn a new skill. Simply having this conversation can set a number of wheels in motion.

- As a manager, make it a point to really talk to your employees and get to know them. Find out what obstacles are impeding them at work. Ask about their career aspirations. It's simple to find out how things are going. You'd be surprised how much you can find out in their answers, both spoken and left unsaid.

- Once a year, undertake a talent review process to assess the potential of your employees, identify developmental opportunities, and look at compensation to determine if it has become a de-motivator instead of a way of rewarding good performance.

- Outline a path to get your employee to the next level, and review the action steps needed to get there. People want to know what it takes to reach the next level or transition to a new role. Once armed with that information, it becomes a motivator.

DISENGAGED EMPLOYEE #3: HOW HARD IS IT TO SAY THANK YOU?

Gary is a human resources manager for A Brand New You, a marketing firm located in New York, and has been in his current role for five years. He's not comfortable tooting his own horn and prefers to let the work speak for itself. He has a wonderful team who respect and admire him, but they all wonder why Gary has gotten so little recognition from senior management. They know he works hard and accomplishes so much, but they have never seen him publicly rewarded for his accomplishments. Gary tells his team that it doesn't matter to him, but they don't believe it.

As a boss, Gary always recognizes and rewards his people for their accomplishments. So why doesn't he get the same from his boss? He works for someone who really doesn't have much respect for the HR function and probably doesn't understand Gary's value and responsibilities. Even though the company requires it once a year, his boss Harold doesn't even offer performance reviews for his direct reports. Harold creates an environment where Gary is left guessing how he is doing in the role and forced to find other ways to feel good about his work. While Gary is paid well for the job he does, sometimes he just wants Harold to show some outward appreciation.

In corporate America, the answer to the question "how hard is it to say thank you" is: VERY HARD. These two little words are among the most difficult things for people to express. Saying thank you is quickly becoming an extinct practice both in society and in the workplace.

The problem begins at the top of the organization and doesn't get much better as it works its way through the hierarchy. CEOs and other top leaders often don't take the time to say thank you and acknowledge the great work of their managers. In these tough economic times, they ask the managers to do more with less. It's easier for them to sit on the executive floor with their doors closed than to walk around and visit with managers and employees.

These same frontline managers, who aren't appreciated themselves tend to pass this bad behavior trait on to their employees. Managers expect people to just do their jobs, and in theory that should be enough, but it isn't. Employees are motivated by achievement and also by recognition. There's a reason why engagement and recognition are often talked about together. Isn't it human nature to want to be acknowledged for doing a good job? It spurs us on to continue at a high level of achievement.

In addition, if you spend every day doing your job well and get no positive feedback, you start to question why you are working so hard. Without consciously meaning to, people who feel under-appreciated begin to disengage from the work and ultimately the workplace.

THE CURE

Recognition doesn't necessarily need to mean money or gifts. It doesn't have to be loud or public either. In fact, some people actually prefer to be recognized privately. It's the old adage of different strokes for different folks. One of the first things a manager should find out from their employees is how they feel about recognition—and what kind is most motivating for them—then follow through when it is earned.

Here are some easy-to-implement recognition tips that should be in a manager's back pocket:

- Start with a recognition strategy that identifies the employee behaviors you want to reinforce. Once managers take the time to do this, they will be more likely to make it a part of their everyday routine.

- Verbally praise your employees for a job well done (privately or in public depending on their preferences), and be specific about the contribution that you are recognizing.

- Handwrite a note of thanks for a job well done. It's so much more meaningful than doing this through an email or quick hallway conversation.

- Give someone a spot award "in the moment" for a job well done—it could be something as simple as a Starbucks gift card or a box of candy or flowers. It's the immediacy that means the most.

- Bring in pizza for the team to celebrate an accomplishment of a goal.

- Create a "graffiti wall" in your work area with a poster board where employees can write notes of thanks or praise for their coworkers.

- Tie a balloon to an employee's chair with a note of thanks.

- Let others in the organization know of the great work your employee did by publicizing it through a company newsletter or intranet site.

- Create a silly department award such as a stuffed animal or toy that gets passed around monthly based on achievement, which the winner can display in their workspace.

DISENGAGED EMPLOYEE #4:
PEOPLE DON'T LEAVE COMPANIES, THEY LEAVE BAD MANAGERS

John is a systems developer for a fast-growing healthcare company in the South called Patient First. He is a genius who can code anything and is always the first person asked to take on a new project. Because of this, he is on overload and working long hours just to keep up. He works best when he is given the deliverable and then left alone to make sure it gets done. For two years, he worked for a manager who was very adept at sizing up what each of the employees needed from her and then managing them accordingly. She knew that John was a self-driven person who didn't need or want a manager who hovered over him. That's why they worked so well together.

About a year ago, John's manager moved to a new role and John received a new supervisor, Sean, who had a very different managerial style. From day one these two clashed because Sean was a micro-manager who wasn't very confident in his own skills and believed that to be effective he had to constantly hover over his people. That definitely didn't sit well with John, especially since he knew he was more technically competent than Sean.

After six months of growing frustration, John asked for a meeting with Sean and tried to express his concern about the working relationship. He offered up some solutions for how it could be better for both of them. Sean didn't want to listen and told John this was how he managed and if he didn't like it, he could find a new job. As John's disenchantment with his job grew, he knew his only chance of staying with the company he loved was to look for another job internally. Thankfully he was able to transfer to a new role with a manager who understood and respected John's skills.

IT'S A FACT

The number one reason employees leave their companies is because of their managers. It's not about compensation or a better opportunity or even a desire to relocate. Every second of every day, an employee is tapped on the shoulder and told, "Congratulations, you are now a manager." The next words out of the employee's mouth usually are: "great, but now what?" Just because you are a good writer or systems developer or financial analyst doesn't mean you have the leadership skills to be a strong manager. No one wakes up the day after being promoted and instantly knows how to provide coaching and feedback, write a performance review, conduct a sexual harassment investigation, or even fire someone. It is sad to note how few resources (both time and dollars) most companies devote to training new managers. And then we wonder why the workplace is filled with bad managers.

While it takes time to develop great leaders, most companies don't feel like they have the luxury to do this. Instead, they thrust ill-prepared managers into stressful workplace environments and take a wait-and-see approach. More times than not, they fail. Unfortunately, many of these bad managers remain in their roles, continuing to lead teams without getting any feedback. So where's the incentive to change?

THE BAD BOSS JOB DESCRIPTION

Bad bosses usually have at least one, if not many, of the following traits:

- They are micro-managers.

- They hide behind closed doors and signal their preference for being unavailable.

- They don't get the concept of "one size does not fit all," and practice only one kind of leadership instead of modifying their behavior based on the needs of their employees.

- They are not effective communicators and tend to keep things hidden from their team.

- They have a reluctance to take action and be decisive, seemingly paralyzed by the fear of making a mistake.

- They are detached from their employees and make no effort to get to know them, their strengths, or their developmental needs.

Given how many different ways bosses can screw up and impact the people working for them, it's no surprise that this is a leading cause of employee disengagement. When you sign on to work for a company, you expect to work for someone who is a leader, has your best interests at heart, and is there to coach you to a high level of performance. When that doesn't happen, the passion you might have had for your job tends to fade out and disengagement sets in.

THE CURE

You *can* fix a bad manager; it just takes time and a bit of work. In particular, frontline managers have one of the most important jobs in any company. There is no better investment an organization can make than in providing its leadership team with basic supervisory skills training. This training should include preparation regarding situational leadership, which is foundational to understanding the readiness level of your employees.

Some people need and want a very direct hands-on approach and others, like John, prefer just to know the end goal and then be left alone to get there. Others are somewhere in between; learning the fine art of assessing your employees is a huge key to becoming a great manager. Many of the skills that make someone a good manager, such as listening, providing clear direction, and making a solid connection with the person working for them, can also be transferable to your life outside of work. A number of core leadership concepts come in handy when raising children or dealing with a life partner.

DISENGAGED EMPLOYEE #5: WOW, IT'S TOXIC IN HERE

Kate knows all too well what it feels like to work for a bully boss. In her twenty-year career, she's had four of them and wonders why she won the lottery when it comes to working for toxic managers. Even though she is a senior executive at a nationwide retailer, The Shirt Shack, her road to the top was paved with many potholes. Kate was subjected to bosses who have humiliated her in front of her peers, stabbed her in the back by taking credit for work she did, undermined her with her own team, and even targeted her with sexist remarks designed to demean her.

Over the years, Kate's confidence plummeted with the abuse from her bully bosses. Even when she finally found the courage to speak to senior management about her current boss, his bosses threw it back in her face by telling her to get a thicker skin and just deal with it. She heard from a colleague (also a woman) that this kind of bullying was commonplace among the men who made up the senior executive team. As she walked back to her office, Kate asked herself, "What is it about me that makes me an easy target for bullies?" She can't stop blaming herself even though she clearly isn't at fault, and she's finding it harder and harder to get engaged in the work any longer.

THE DIRTY LITTLE SECRET CORPORATE AMERICA DOESN'T WANT OUT

Bullying is such an overwhelming issue in the workplace and in life. Every day we see a different news story about someone being bullied around the world. In 2010, a Rutgers University student named Tyler Clementi killed himself after being bullied by his roommate and his friends who spied on his personal encounters via a webcam. In 2012, elementary school students bullied a sixty-eight-year-old school bus monitor named Karen Klein. When the video and story went viral, strangers around the world reacted by pledging over $700,000 in donations for her so she could quit her job. She used $100,000 as seed money to start the Karen Klein Anti-Bullying Foundation. In 2013, two girls in Florida (one twelve and the other fourteen) were arrested and charged with bullying a fellow classmate who eventually committed suicide because of how she was treated. The list goes on and on.

These stories and many others are splashed all over the media. So why haven't we heard more about the proliferation of bullying in corporate America? Even though the largest percentage of bullying today takes place in the workplace, no one ever wants to talk about it. It's the big secret corporations don't want revealed. The number of workers bullied on the job is staggering. The incredibly sad part is: no one seems to want to do anything to address this crisis.

Bullies come in all sizes and flavors, and many of us have sampled at least one of them. Here are just a few of the types of bullies that flourish in the workplace:

THE INTIMIDATOR

This kind of bully thrives on using intimidating words to make sure that his dislike of someone is both heard and felt. He uses the "perceived power" of his role to justify that it's okay to talk down to people. He threatens his targets, either implicitly or overtly, that if they don't do what he wants then it will harm their careers. Intimidators are actually inflicted with their own disease, that of low self-esteem.

THE SEXIST

This is a boss who revels in treating someone of the opposite sex as inferior. More often than not, this is a male superior who bullies a female subordinate by saying things like "women don't belong in senior roles," "a man can do this job better," or "if you are a good girl and say pretty please." Comments such as these are intended to demean the employee and lower their confidence level. These kinds of comments have no place in today's work environment.

THE SCAB PICKER

Do you remember a time when you fell down and scraped your knee? As it healed, a scab formed on the cut. How many times did you pick at that scab because it itched? If you did, the result caused the cut to bleed more, right? That same concept happens with bullies. The scab picker is a person who can see that something is a sore spot for their target. Instead of leaving him alone, they pick at him until the wound opens up again. Like a laser beam, they focus in again and again on the same spot, ensuring that true healing can never take place.

THE SCREAMER

This is what most people identify with when they hear the word bully. The common tactic of a screamer bully boss is to be the loudest voice in the room, falsely assuming that this kind of behavior will ensure results, which it doesn't. These bullies are loud, obnoxious, and abusive and have but one goal: to berate and humiliate people in public. They thrive on the notion that others fear them. In fact, most screamers are suffering from low self-confidence and insecurity, and they try to mask it by being the loudest, meanest person in the room.

THE TWO-FACED SNAKE IN THE GRASS

Bosses aren't the only bullies in the workplace. Your colleagues can be just as bad. This bully is someone who says one thing to your face and the opposite behind your back. In many instances, they are complaining to you about your mutual boss while at the same time undermining you with that same manager. They are the first to destroy your reputation, stab you in the back, and take all the credit for the work they haven't done.

THE CURE

Concentrate solely on your work and dedicating yourself to getting out from under your abuser and not letting yourself become a target.

Approach your bullying problem like a daily task by being methodical in how you behave, perform on the job, and document what's going on. Stay calm and unemotional at all times.

- Display self-esteem and show a positive attitude, and don't give your bully the satisfaction of seeing how this is affecting you.

- Don't let yourself become isolated from others in the workplace. Take a moment each and every day to find someone you haven't recently talked to and make a connection. Bullies love to alienate their targets among their coworkers.

- Remain calm and quiet, which can throw a bully off his game. Yelling back is never the answer. During a bullying session find a way to excuse yourself from the situation by citing another meeting or a need to use the restroom. Even a few minutes away can calm the situation.

- Don't rely solely on human resources personnel; they are very rarely the people who can stop a bully, and in fact some have been known to be bullies themselves.

- Create a "get out" strategy, because usually bullies won't stop their behavior. It's better for you to take control over your life than to rely on others to change.

It's a lot easier to solve a problem when you know what the "it" is. The first step to reengaging in work and in life is admitting what's at the root of the disengagement. More times than not, the root is identifiable and easy to recognize. It may start with that feeling of lacking satisfaction and fulfillment and slowly transform into resentment and a deep-seated emotional disconnect from your job.

Remember the example of the tree with the rotten roots. On the outside you may appear healthy. But on the inside you are feeling smothered, encompassed by a negative boss and a poisonous environment. Eventually the outside will match the inside. The roots will grow and the tree will become weak, unable to stand on its own. Eventually the tree will lose its leaves and die. The goal is to stop the roots from decaying and create an environment that promotes nourishment and substantial growth. Together, our journey will help you to realize the fruits are in the roots.

Chapter Three

THE SYMPTOMS OF DISENGAGEMENT

*H*ow do you know when you have a dead tree in your yard? Have the branches stopped growing? Are the leaves yellow or brown instead of a rich shade of green? Is the grass surrounding the base of the tree patchy and dried out?

Mother Nature does a great job of showing the direct correlation between all kinds of elements. While sunshine nourishes the grass, shrubs, and trees, without water they stand no chance to survive. The scarcity of healthy grass can then negatively impact the animals that rely on it for nourishment. It's a harmonious process whereby things feed off one another for both sustainability and growth.

Nothing in nature can exist in a vacuum and without a direct connection to other living elements. At times Mother Nature can disrupt the harmony of the environment by wreaking havoc through vicious storms, extreme temperatures, and plenty of other natural disasters. Although damage is done along the way, eventually the cycle of life (and nature) rebalances itself and everything is reborn and revitalized.

WHAT DOES MOTHER NATURE HAVE TO DO WITH DISENGAGEMENT?

The same interconnected cycle of life that we see in nature is evident in the disease of disengagement. The pieces of the puzzle consistently feed off each other and ultimately impact others around us. In the last chapter we discussed the underlying causes of disengagement and how many of these causes are easily interconnected. For example, if you have a bad boss you are likely not getting the recognition and appreciation you need to be nourished and engaged in the work. If you feel stuck in your job, it wouldn't be surprising to hear that your job isn't exactly what was promised when you started.

But take this one step further. Consider the notion that what occurs in the workplace can impact your personal life and vice versa. These two worlds feed off each other and either come together in a joyous abundance of engagement, or collide in a dismal bout of disengagement. The crossover between work and home can't be ignored.

If you are experiencing problems at home such as marital or financial issues, it is likely that this stress also joins you every day in the workplace. Conversely, if you are dealing with a bully boss and feeling unappreciated, you can't help but bring that disengagement home with you. It's a pretty impossible task to compartmentalize your life. Just like Mother Nature, everything is interconnected.

FORGET WORK/LIFE BALANCE—IT'S ALL ABOUT THE LIFE/WORK COLLISION COURSE

So many of our actions are not intentional but rather happen because of circumstances that may be out of our control. If you've had a bad day at work, it's difficult to flip the switch and walk in the door of your home happy and carefree. When your kids jump on you wanting to play is your reaction to join in, or is it to first have some quiet downtime? If your wife has prepared a romantic dinner for the two of you, are you able to clear your mind and enjoy it, or would you rather just eat in silence in front of the TV?

On the flipside, if you are dealing with issues in your marriage and spent the evening arguing with your spouse, are you then able to joyfully awake in the morning with a clear head and embrace the day ahead? The skeptics might argue that work can be a sanctuary and a place where you can focus on other things. Truth be told, you can't really leave your cares at the office door; it just doesn't happen. If you are happy and engaged at work, then you are better positioned to address the issues in your personal life. However, it will only serve to make your personal struggles that much harder to handle if you are unhappy and disengaged at work.

We don't always recognize that we are wearing our employee disengagement like a scarlet letter. Picture someone dealing with a bad manager in the workplace who goes to play basketball with a bunch of friends over the weekend. Without meaning to, he plays aggressively by running roughshod over his friends. Why? Subconsciously he is fighting back against the bully boss.

Another example is the spouse who is unhappy at work and comes home sad and withdrawn, unwilling to share his day's events. His spouse has no idea why he doesn't smile anymore and thinks it's because of something she did. Disengagement intersects with your personal life and can either disrupt harmony or suck the life out of you.

During my journey, numerous people have shared their personal disengagement stories. While the names have been changed to protect the innocent (and guilty), all the stories are real. Throughout this book I'll be sharing some of these with you so that you can "look in the mirror" to see yourself in them.

ANN'S STORY

BLOWING IN THE WIND

Your first impression of Ann is usually how tall and athletic she is, topped off by her infectious smile. You can't help but look up when she walks by and connect with her individuality. What you don't see is the internal pain she is struggling to understand. After a long and successful career in the music industry, Ann woke up to a loud drumbeat pulsing in her head that said, "You've mastered this, now what?"

While her feet were still on the ground, her head and heart were feeling detached from her body, no longer anchored in their rightful place. The scars from a recent divorce were still fresh enough to be raw. Ann told me that the deeper meaning of the work she always relished was fading away and that she no longer enjoyed the sweet perks of the music industry she used to treasure. She used to enjoy activities like going to amazing music festivals such as South by Southwest and Coachella. But now she feels like they have become chores. Swaying to the music with friends and colleagues now felt like being in a pit full of sweaty people stepping on her toes to get closer to the stage. Instead of staying out late, she couldn't wait to get back to her room to be alone with her thoughts.

One day, another in a series of life-changing moments for Ann came when a realtor said that houses in her neighborhood were selling like crazy. Without stepping back and rationally thinking things through, Ann decided to put her house on the market. She quickly sold her home, and the rest of her possessions followed shortly thereafter. Around the same time, the band she was managing for over seventeen years called and indicated they couldn't afford her services any longer. As the blood rushed out of her head, Ann's inner voice said, "Wow, this is scary, but the fear is colored with moments of excitement." Ann knew life was indeed about to change.

In a period of reflection and clarity, Ann acknowledged that she had been disengaged—both at work and in life, feeling stripped down to her birthday suit and completely exposed. When sharing these events and her innermost thoughts with me, she described it as standing at the edge of the ocean and feeling like a gust of wind would blow her into the water.

WHAT ARE THE SYMPTOMS OF ENGAGEMENT?

To fully understand the symptoms of disengagement, it helps to first talk about the characteristics of someone who is fully engaged—in work and/or in life. Sometimes it is easier to understand why a tree dies by studying one that is healthy and flourishing. While these symptoms are geared to the workplace, you can see how easily they translate to one's personal life as well.

- Committed
- Loyal
- Energetic
- Creative
- Open to change
- Willing to take risks

Engaged people are truly committed to what they are doing. With commitment comes a sense of loyalty to those in their lives, both at a professional and a personal level. It takes energy to be engaged. You can't successfully do your job without putting forth effort. The same goes for being in a relationship or raising children. Engaged people are creative and open to change. They aren't satisfied with the status quo. It requires courage to take risks, but great reward comes with doing so. It's risky to get married or have children, but also to reach for a goal at work.

SYMPTOMS OF INDIVIDUAL DISENGAGEMENT IN THE WORKPLACE

Disengagement can manifest itself in many ways. There are symptoms exhibited by individual employees suffering from disengagement. Then there are symptoms exhibited by organizations with a high percentage of disengaged employees throughout their ranks.

They are different yet related. So let's explore this further by detailing what exactly to look for.

Here are some symptoms that frequently show up in disengaged employees:

I Don't Care Attitude. These employees have given up on even making a pretense of caring about the work. They show up and do what is expected but don't expend energy to make sure the work is high quality. It's all about just getting it done, not about getting it done right.

Increased Absences or Tardiness. Disengaged employees have trouble getting up in the morning and arriving at work on time. They show up when they want, not when they are scheduled to be there. They tend to suffer more than their engaged colleagues with stress-induced illnesses. These symptoms could be as small as a headache or cold, but as large as depression, anxiety, or deep sadness.

Declining Quality of Work. Employees who used to care about the quality of their work and paid attention to small details no longer have the energy to do so. They simply don't care if all the i's are dotted and the t's are crossed. It's more about just checking the box and moving on to the next task. Error rates increase when employees are not engaged in the job at hand, and work is done at a slower pace.

Mood Swings. Is today a good day or a bad one? People who are disengaged tend to have more mood swings than others. Usually they wear their emotions on their face. It gets harder and harder for them to hide their moods, and they prefer to just go with their feelings. They don't care if others notice because how they feel is how they show up.

Isolating Themselves From Others. Isolation can take two forms. One can be intentional, where the disengaged employee chooses to opt out. That happens a lot in larger group settings. Someone sits back and does not participate in the conversation. They don't join in hallway conversations or at the local lunch joint with the rest of the team. The second way it can show up is in their own heads. In this form, disengaged employees feel like they are invisible, even in a very visible role. They believe others ignore them in the group, even if there is no validity to this feeling.

No Creativity or Input. Something happens when a person falls into disengagement. They suddenly appear to become mute. A once deafening voice is seemingly nonexistent. They make the choice to stay silent and don't offer their input or advice, even when asked directly to do so. They stop being creative and trying new things. They retreat to the familiar and routine and do everything they can to stay under the radar.

Lethargic. You can usually tell when someone crosses over from engagement into disengagement by focusing on their energy level. When it comes to how people show up on a daily basis, there is a marked change in behavior. All of their movements slow down and things seem to move at a snail's pace. Even Type A personalities are not immune from this telltale sign, and in fact, with them it's even more noticeable.

SYMPTOMS OF ORGANIZATIONAL DISENGAGEMENT IN THE WORKPLACE

Some of the symptoms present in an individual suffering from disengagement show up organizationally as well. They just take on a different look and feel when it involves more than one person. Here are some of the challenges facing a disengaged workplace:

Lack of Creativity. Organizations with a high level of disengagement tend to shy away from new ideas, preferring instead to stay with the tried-and-true way of doing business. They are not innovative or creative. They don't recognize and reward their employees for coming up with new products or processes. There's no incentive to step out of the box and challenge the status quo.

Unwilling to Take Risks. These organizations are risk-averse and not comfortable stepping out of their comfort zones. In companies with high engagement, it's not uncommon to see people actually rewarded for failing so long as they took a risk and tried something new. In disengaged companies, you can get punished for the same kind of behaviors. Great organizations are usually those that at some point took a shot on a new product or way of doing something, knowing full well it had a chance to backfire on them.

Resistant to Change. Just as disengaged organizations are unwilling to color outside the lines, it's no surprise that the next symptom is a resistance to change. It's all about remaining in the box and going through the motions. Change is risky by nature and brings uncertainty into the proceedings. Going through change usually requires more energy and work than a disengaged organization is willing to commit to.

High Turnover. If people are struggling with the underlying causes of disengagement (as outlined in the previous chapter), the easy way out is to just quit. Unhappy employees vote with their feet. Turnover is one of the best metrics to assess employees' satisfaction with companies. In fact, high turnover in a time of tough economic conditions worldwide should be a huge red flag to an organization that something is just not right.

Low Customer Satisfaction. How employees feel about their jobs shows up in the level of service they provide to their customers. In fact, a number of companies are now correlating their employee engagement survey results to their customer satisfaction metrics to validate this theory. Customers can tell when the representatives they are talking to in a call center or working with at a retail store are unhappy at their job. It shows up in their energy level, mannerisms, and voice and how willing they are to resolve your problem.

Increased Safety Issues. A lack of energy and attention, common symptoms of disengaged employees, can have a disastrous impact on safety in the workplace. Manufacturing companies that have low engagement scores usually have a correlating high rate of safety issues. Organizations with a large percentage of employees who have an "I don't care" attitude pay little to no attention to rules and procedures designed to protect them from an unsafe environment. This issue also plays out in retail organizations by an increased level of theft. Shoplifters prey on companies that have distracted and unresponsive employees.

SILENCE IS NOT GOLDEN

In the case of disengaged employees, silence is just a false front. As a coping mechanism, disengaged people have gotten good at smiling on the outside while crying on the inside. It's amazing the lengths people go to sometimes just to get through the day. The following story is a great illustration of this.

BETH'S STORY

ACTING OUT

I've known Beth for a long time now, as we worked together on numerous philanthropic initiatives. The first thing that strikes you when you meet her is how poised and professional she is, always in control and impeccably put together. When she walks into a room, people look her way and smile in admiration. Along with her nonprofit work, Beth was a top executive at a prestigious local organization, seemingly at the top of her game in all facets of her life.

One day I ran into her husband and he asked what I was doing these days. I mentioned that I was writing a book on disengagement in the workplace and highlighting the underlying causes of this disease, including bullying. He turned to me and said, "You need to talk to my wife; she has quite a story to share." I tried not to let the shock show on my face. Not the woman I knew, no way!

I took Beth to lunch, and what I learned was that her boss was a classic bully who employed tactics designed to demean and zap the confidence of others that weren't in her inner circle. When asked to describe how she felt in the workplace, Beth sighed and said she was sad, emotional, and felt just plain awful. I told her that she didn't show this on the outside and asked what her secret was.

The answer she gave caused me to smile. It seems that Beth's outlet for her disengagement and pain was to take an improvisational acting class. It's hard to see this elegant, reserved, and professional woman performing improvisational comedy in front of a group of strangers. After I regained my composure, I asked her why she decided to do this. Her answer: "It taught me to remove myself from the pain by becoming someone else" in the workplace.

There is no way Beth's colleagues could have diagnosed her with disengagement based on the symptoms covered earlier in this chapter. She went out of her way to keep her secret, but at what cost to her?

HONEY, I'M HOME

Do you simply leave the pain behind, or do you take it with you once the workday is over and it's time to go home or meet up with friends? If you take it with you (which is not a choice, it just happens), how does it show up in a different, more personal setting? There's not a dial in your brain where you can just switch to a new channel and have a different loop play in your head. It takes time to transition from one set of feelings to another.

No matter how long or short your commute is, it is never long enough to clear your mind if you are mired in a state of disengagement. This is the same if you drive to work and try to forget about the fight you just had with your partner or the stack of never-ending bills that are piled high on your desk. Entering the workplace won't magically get rid of those thoughts. Conversely, if you spent eight hours trying to cope with your bully boss who decided you were his favorite target today, you probably won't spend your commute home singing along with the radio.

How do you just "snap out of it" (whatever *it* is) when you transition between work and home? How do you hold back the resentment that might be bubbling to the surface when all you want to do is be alone with your feelings and not interact with others who always expect you to be upbeat and connected? One of the first steps is to acknowledge that *what's happening at work is impacting you on a personal level as well.*

Here are some symptoms that show up in people who bring the pain of disengagement to the workplace or back home with them:

Disconnecting From People Who Love You. People who are disengaged often try to hide their pain from their loved ones because they think they are doing them a favor by not bringing it home with them. Unfortunately, not even the greatest magician can pull off that trick. While your loved ones may not know the specifics or the depth of your pain, they know something is off. They may jump to conclusions and think they did something wrong to cause your unhappiness. This can bring on stress in even the best marriages. It's even worse with your kids, who are often too young to understand why Daddy doesn't want to play with them. They've waited all day to see you, and no amount of explanation can ease the pain of a child rejected by a parent.

Aggravation and Aggression. It's helpful to have an outlet for the pain when you are tired of keeping your feelings bottled up. A lot of people go to the gym to exercise their demons away. But things may go awry when you push yourself harder than your body can take simply to numb the pain. That bottled-up aggression can also come out on the basketball court or baseball diamond, and since your friends don't know what's going on inside your head, they might get unintentionally hurt by your actions.

No Enjoyment Anymore. It's easier to stay home getting lost in your playlist or playing remote-control roulette on your television than it is to interact with others. Even something as simple as sharing a romantic dinner with your partner can feel like a chore.

Substance Abuse. One of the most overused coping mechanisms for people struggling with disengagement and unhappiness is self-medication, either through alcohol or drugs. It's the quickest numbing agent around but also the one with the most lasting side effects. If your loved one comes home and immediately heads to the bar to fix a drink, it may be a flashing neon sign of something painful and deep-seated.

THE EYES HAVE IT

Noah Alper, author of Business Mensch: Timeless Wisdom for Today's Entrepreneur, *and the founder of the Noah's Bagels chain, recently told me that he could walk into any of his stores and immediately know if that particular location had engaged employees. While he had statistics such as turnover to identify potential issues, for him the answer was in the eyes. He could see if there was energy happening, a buzz, if you will. If he walked in and the music was too loud, the display cases were askew, or his employees were dressed inappropriately then he was dealing with a disengaged store. To Noah, it was the intangibles. Energy is either there or it isn't; it just feels flat.*

Symptoms are just one piece of the puzzle, but the true test comes when you can determine the existence of disengagement by diagnosing the extent of the problem. Let's dig deeper into that in the next chapter.

Chapter Four

DIAGNOSING DISENGAGEMENT

*T*hink about the leaves on our tree turning brown and shedding at an alarming rate. Your first thought may be that the roots are indeed rotten. Or how about if your significant other comes home from work with a sad face and retreats to his favorite room in the house, closes the door, and makes little effort to communicate with you. You wonder if you did something wrong. But similar to the tree succumbing to seasonal change rather than rotting roots, your loved one may just be coping with the ever-present disengagement he is experiencing at work. Really, it has nothing to do with you.

As any doctor can tell you, accurately diagnosing a disease can be a very difficult thing to do. Many of the same symptoms are present in a variety of diseases, and it's easy to confuse one ailment for another. The presumed problem may not be the problem at all. Only when you do additional diagnostics designed to prove the accuracy of your original hypothesis does the answer become clear. If even a well-trained doctor finds difficulty in diagnosing an ailment, you can only imagine the confusion a loved one experiences when trying to understand and assess someone's level of engagement.

WHICH CAME FIRST, THE CHICKEN OR THE EGG?

It's not uncommon for one disease to mimic another. If an individual shows some of the symptoms we discussed in the prior chapter, like feeling lethargic, trouble awakening in the morning, and constant isolation, you may initially think he is depressed. But the truth is he could also be disengaged. Because many of the symptoms overlap, the ailments can be muddled. There may even be simultaneous issues occurring. You can feel unfulfilled and lack purpose in your life if you are depressed. That can lead to poor performance at work, fights with your loved ones, unhealthy eating habits, and an overall desire not to care for your body or your life. The point is that it's easy to misdiagnose this as disengagement.

As comparison, according to the National Institute of Mental Health (NIMH), here are some of the key symptoms of depression:

- Difficulty concentrating, remembering details, and making decisions
- Fatigue and decreased energy
- Feelings of guilt, worthlessness, and/or helplessness
- Feelings of hopelessness and/or pessimism
- Insomnia
- Irritability and restlessness
- Loss of interest in hobbies or activities once pleasurable

Many of these symptoms appear in the disengaged individual as well. You could only imagine how much confusion this creates for loved ones looking in from the outside. In fact, the disengaged person probably feels depressed as well and confused as to which symptom is linked to which disease. So which is it? Which came first? Are the two connected?

ANXIOUS MOMENTS

Does suffering from anxiety disorders predispose you to falling prey to disengagement? If you are disengaged, does that bring about anxiety? Much like depression, anxiety is one of those diseases that can be directly linked to how engaged you are in both your personal and professional life.

According to NIMH, here are some of the symptoms people with anxiety disorders experience:

- Feelings of panic, fear, and uneasiness
- Nightmares
- Problems sleeping
- Palpitations
- Repeated thoughts/flashbacks of traumatic situations
- Avoidance of social situations

Sometimes your symptoms may seem to indicate depression or anxiety, but the reality is you are disengaged in your daily work responsibilities. It's not unusual to have symptoms that mimic others, which makes the diagnostic process even more critical. The key is to be able to diagnose the malady correctly and in a timely manner.

DIGGING DEEP

There is always a causal relationship between leading an unhealthy lifestyle and your overall health. An overweight person doesn't pack on the pounds when living a healthy lifestyle. People don't just wake up one day and decide to gain weight. Any good trainer can work with you on the physical aspect of burning calories, but the more critical need is to get inside someone's head to find out what is driving his unhealthy behavior. Many experts believe behaviors or circumstances cannot change until an individual acknowledges what got him in a particular position. It is those behavioral norms or subconscious programs that created the problem in the first place.

Typically you don't hear an overweight person stand up in public and shout: "Hey, I figured it out, I'm disengaged." But it's clear that many of his eating issues could stem from related problems that could ultimately lead to this diagnosis. Many overweight people talk about being bullied or teased, feeling the pain from a lost love, failures in their personal or professional lives, and even serious abandonment issues. They often retreat to their homes, live solitary lives, and eat to mask the pain of the outside world. If asked, some of them might admit to suffering from some form of disengagement at a specific point in time.

Overeating is just a symptom of the bigger problem. Symptoms on top of symptoms mimic disease after disease. With so many layers, what's an individual to think? And since many diseases mimic others, how can we truly diagnose the presence of disengagement?

THE OUTDATED ACT OF DIAGNOSING EMPLOYEE ENGAGEMENT

As we stated in chapter one, employee engagement isn't a new concept; it's been around since the 1920s when researchers studied morale and a group's willingness to accomplish organizational objectives. It really became relevant in the late '80s when a number of researchers focused their attention on job satisfaction and organization commitment. The Gallup Organization then took this a step further when they rolled out their Q12 survey instrument focused solely on employee engagement. Many other organizations have jumped on the bandwagon and introduced their own engagement survey tools.

Way back when (okay, it was only the '80s), if a company wanted to know how their employees were feeling, they conducted an employee satisfaction survey. This was generally a lengthy (sixty-five-plus questions) survey that covered a wide range of subjects including, but not limited to, the following areas:

- Teamwork

- Mission and purpose

- Senior leadership

- Direct manager

- Opportunities for growth

- Quality and customer focus

- Pay and benefits

- Feedback

These kinds of surveys are exhausting, both to take and to interpret. It's information overload of the highest order. For me, the most comical questions were always in the compensation section. How many of us are inclined to answer yes when asked: "Are you paid fairly for the work you do?" Unless you own the company, you probably feel you are worth much more than you are getting paid.

Closely tied for that dubious title is the question that asks, "Do you believe the results from this survey will be followed up on in a timely manner?" This question never fails to meet with cynical laughter and rather low scores.

The other problem with this type of survey is that it's unfocused. The data gatherers end up with a slew of opportunities to improve employee satisfaction but not enough hours in the day to get it all done. Be careful what you wish for, right?

Another factor that doomed these kinds of surveys is the long cycle time from the development of the survey to its administration to the publishing of the results to holding focus groups to confirm the findings and finally the action plan to fix them. In most cases a good six months elapsed before the answers presented themselves. Since most companies did these surveys on an annual basis, it was time for the next one not long after they received the results. It became a vicious cycle of constant survey taking with little-to-no real action in between.

Employee satisfaction surveys are cumbersome, unfocused, and time consuming in a day when we do everything in sound bites (Twitter anyone?). You really can't get more old school than this.

ENTER GALLUP, THE TWO-TON GORILLA

While many other organizations specialize in employee engagement survey tools, the clear leader in this field is The Gallup Organization. Founded in 1935, the company started with an original focus on market research and public-opinion polling. In 1988 Gallup was purchased by a company called Selection Research Inc. that gave them a worldwide reach, as they branched out to measuring customer satisfaction.

In the late 1990s, as the business environment became even more global and competitive, Gallup implemented a new strategy and direction to understand the opinions of employees regarding their employers. Gallup took advantage of the desire of corporate leaders to study employee attitudes that affected workplace morale and overall productivity. Gallup was clearly in the right place at the right time to provide a tool that was much more focused and user-friendly than the outdated employee satisfaction surveys.

Gallup strengthened their hold on the employee engagement marketplace with their Q12 survey instrument and bestselling books such as *First, Break All the Rules* and *Now, Discover Your Strengths* as accompanying companion tools. Finally, companies could administer a survey that focused on the right things and was easy to understand. Along with the bestselling Strength Finders tool, no one could touch Gallup when it came to employee engagement. Given all this, why is even this cutting-edge company old news?

While the Gallup tool is still an effective way to measure employee engagement, here's what ultimately led to the creation of a more conscious and relevant disengagement diagnostic tool. From a process standpoint, there still remains a long period of time between administration of the survey and delivery of the results to the employees who participated. In our fast-paced business world, even six months is too long. The cost of administering the survey is very expensive and can be prohibitive for small to midsize companies.

But that's not even the biggest problem with the survey. Gallup suggests you should only pay attention to the "top box" score when reviewing the survey results—the percentage of employees who were actually highly engaged. In reality, surveyors should be much more concerned with the percentage of employees who identify themselves as actively disengaged. That is the single most important metric, as this is the group with the most impact on the success or failure of any organization.

TAKE MY PULSE, PLEASE

With the time it took for results to cascade down the organization, managers grew tired of waiting for what turned out to be old data. They wanted to know, on a timelier basis, how their employees were currently feeling. Under previous practices, by the time they found out an employee was disengaged, it was too late. They wanted to react more effectively. Why wait to hear how engaged your people are in a social-media-crazed world where at any second you can post your feelings on Twitter, Facebook, Instagram, and other sites?

In 1999, companies like Survey Monkey and Zoomerang popped up to take advantage of people's appetite for real-time information. These quickly became popular tools companies used to target a specific population on a very focused issue. Since you could get the data back the same day, they solved the timeliness issue. But the problem that still exists with these tools today is that the reporting mechanisms and ability to classify information by a variety of different factors is still clunky at best. When it comes to reports and metrics, you don't get the "pretty factor" that vendors such as Gallup previously nailed. But these became your go-to tools of choice if you wanted to get a snapshot in real time on a particular subject

What this doesn't work well with is the individual perspective. When managers use this tool, it is sent to a group of people and then sold on the basis of confidentiality so people will feel free to provide honest feedback. But what if you just want to know about one person in particular? Then what instrument do you use?

TAKE A WALK

You can't get more old-fashioned than the long used "Management by Walking Around" (MBWA) methodology of seeing what's going on with your employees. For decades this has been a useful tactic for managers as a way to gauge the happiness and productivity of their employees. Walk through the bullpen of a call center and you can see if people are busily talking on the phone to customers in an upbeat and engaged manner or just sitting in their chairs wasting the day away. Spend time on the selling floor of a department store and you can quickly assess if the associates are happy to be serving customers.

MBWA encourages leaders to get out of their offices and mingle with their employees. However, one thing it can't do is prepare managers for what to look for. Now that we've gone over the major symptoms of disengagement in the workplace, it might be easier for a manager to walk around and be more clued in to the hunt. While this approach is a start, it doesn't always lend itself to a more in-depth look at an individual person.

YOU CAN BE INVISIBLE, EVEN IN A VERY VISIBLE ROLE

Whether at work or at home, many people suffering from disengagement share a common trait: they feel invisible around others. It doesn't matter if you're a secretary, a CFO, a nurse, or a stay-at-home wife and mother; you can still feel like no one knows you are there or even cares about how you feel. I felt that way—so much so that I thought about why others couldn't "see" my feelings. Both at work and at home, I realized that others around me just didn't know the right questions to ask to assess my state of being.

Dissatisfaction with the old-fashioned way of thinking led me to create the Invisibility Index Tool™ to diagnose disengagement. This tool can be used at the workplace or at home to help identify disengagement disease.

Currently there are two versions of the Invisibility Index™. The first is for managers to use to assess the engagement level of their employees. The second index is designed to be a self-assessment tool for anyone trying to understand the feelings going on inside themselves.

By focusing on a series of questions regarding normal and everyday occurrences as well as the frequency of the behavior, this tool can get someone started on the path to recovery and reengagement. These indexes are simply a jumping-off point from which to further probe. It's all about spotting the behavior and digging deeper to see if there is a pattern that shows disengagement.

Here are the two tools:

Invisibility Index™

Manager Assessment Version

For each statement below, check the box that most closely describes your assessment of the employee

	Statement	Always	Frequently	Some-times	Once in a While	Never
1.	My employee is showing an increase in absenteeism, tardiness, and/or leaving early					
2.	My employee takes longer lunches and breaks					
3.	My employee makes negative comments about their work, management, and/or the organization					
4.	My employee is disconnected from me and/or their colleagues					
5.	My employee shows little initiative or interest in work					

6. My employee shows a lack of creativity and innovation					
7. My employee shows a lack of trust in management, becoming more suspicious or paranoid					
8. My employee misses deadlines, fails to meet commitments					
9. My employee is quick to get angry over small annoyances					
10. My employee resists collaborating on tasks that require teamwork					
11. My employee works against quality or safety standards, organizational policies and procedures, or company rules and regulations					
12. My employee refuses to talk about his or her future in the organization					

13. My employee undermines or criticizes the contributions of others					
14. My employee no longer provides input in group meetings					
15. My employee shows no interest in learning new things or attending training					
16. My employee is not paying attention to customer needs or service quality					
17. My employee spends more time assessing blame than finding solutions					
18. My employee shuts themselves off from colleagues, doesn't seem to have a best friend at work they can trust					
19. My employee doesn't participate in or encourage recognition of others or team celebrations					

20. My employee doesn't come to me with concerns, suggestions, or new ideas					

SCORING SYSTEM

Use the following point system for each question. Add up all your points.

Always	5 points
Frequently	4 points
Sometimes	3 points
Once in a While	2 points
Never	1 point

IS YOUR EMPLOYEE DISENGAGED?

1 to 40 points   You have a healthy, engaged employee who is a role model for others in the organization

41 to 60 points   You have identified the disengagement disease in its earliest stages and may not need much effort to get rid of the symptoms and quickly reengage your employee

61 to 80 points   Your employee is in stage three of the disease and may not yet be terminal, but treatment should begin soon

81 to 100 points   Your employee is in critical condition and the disengagement disease is nearing stage four; immediate treatment required

Invisibility Index™
Self-Assessment Version

For each statement below, check the box that most closely describes you

Statement	Always	Frequently	Some-times	Once in a While	Never
1. I have trouble getting up to go to work and have an overwhelming feeling of fatigue					
2. I feel sick at the thought of going in to work					
3. I have had more absences than usual or a pattern of coming in to work late and/or leaving early					
4. I am making negative comments about my work, management, and/or the organization					
5. I feel disconnected from my manager and/or my colleagues					

6. I have been showing little initiative or interest in work					
7. I am exhibiting a lack of creativity and innovation					
8. I have a lack of trust in management, becoming more suspicious or paranoid					
9. I am missing deadlines and failing to meet commitments					
10. I am quick to get angry over small annoyances					
11. I resist collaborating on tasks that require teamwork					
12. I am spending more time assessing blame than finding solutions					
13. I find myself working against quality or safety standards, organizational policies and procedures, or company rules and regulations					

14. I have undermined or criticized the contributions of others					
15. I no longer provide input in group meetings					
16. I have no interest in learning new things or attending training					
17. I don't pay attention to customer needs or service quality					
18. I shut myself off from colleagues and don't have a best friend at work I can trust					
19. I don't participate in or encourage recognition of others or team celebrations					
20. I don't go to my manager with concerns, suggestions, or new ideas					

SCORING

Use the following point system for each question. Add up all your points.

Always:	5 points
Frequently:	4 points
Sometimes:	3 points
Once in a While:	2 points
Never:	1 point

ARE YOU DISENGAGED?

1 to 40 points	Congratulations, you are fully engaged and happy and serve as a role model for others
41 to 60 points	You are engaged but not 100 percent committed to your job or organization and are keeping an eye on those things that concern you
61 to 80 points	You are showing the warning signs of disengagement and need a spark to reengage your flame before it's too late
81 to 100 points	This is a wakeup call that you have contracted the disengagement disease and are in need of immediate treatment

THE SPOUSE AND FRIEND TEST

While these two questionnaires are designed more for the workplace, the concepts can easily be adjusted for issues occurring at home. In particular, when administering a self-assessment you can change some of the questions to things like:

- I have trouble leaving my personal issues at home and not bringing them into work with me

- I don't want to go out with friends after work or on the weekend

- I just want to come home and have private time before engaging with my family

- When I work out or play sports I am much more aggressive than I should be

- I have no interest in romance with my significant other

- I snap at my children for no reason at all

While there are many other potential questions/statements to be considered, you can easily see how asking simple questions can help you face the truth about engagement, in both your life and at work. As I've met people on this journey through engagement, some were clueless regarding their own disengagement and others saw it to be as clear as water—they didn't need to be hit over the head with the diagnosis. Consider the story of May, who self-diagnosed her own disengagement disease.

MAY'S STORY

READY TO BURST

When I asked May how long she had been feeling disengaged, her first answer was "I'm going through this now." Before I could get out my next question, she choked off a wry laugh and said, "Looking back, I think it's been going on all seven years here, stemming from soulless work." She actually felt a sense of unease dating back to her first day on the job when she went home that night and told herself, "This work just isn't my passion." Tamping down those feelings, and giving in to her fears,

May stayed—hopefully for only a limited time—but just for the money she desperately needed.

It wasn't the work that caused these feelings of disengagement per se, but more the feeling that she was not where she was supposed to be. While she went about doing her job with a smile on her face, her inner voice kept saying, "This isn't right." May felt like she had developed Attention Deficit Disorder (ADD) in her current role because her body needed, in fact craved, movement. She couldn't seem to focus. For May, the underlying cause of disengagement was a strong feeling that her job didn't align with her core values—the essence of who she is.

As she searched to name her feelings and how to deal with the overwhelming sadness across the years, she talked to friends, hired coaches, learned new skills, and most importantly built an escape route. But she still felt angst and isolation. Finally, she approached her boss and indicated she was about to blow like a volcano. That was the catalyst for change. May knew it was time to listen to her inner voice and leave this job when the right opportunity presented itself. Although she hasn't left yet, the fact that she has an escape plan has made the waiting so much easier, just knowing there is an out.

May's message to others struggling with this disease is to know you are not alone, don't give up on your dream, keep the faith, and it will eventually lead you to a sunnier side of the street.

OLD VERSUS NEW: THE DIAGNOSTIC DILEMMA

Our diagnostic journey from the past to the present can be summarized by the following key takeaways:

- Old school is surveying on everything but new school is targeting key issues

- Old school is looking to create actions for the results from dated survey tools versus a new school approach to create a reaction plan for real-time issues

- Prognosis not diagnosis; let's focus on the likely outcome versus identifying the problem

- Forward-thinking approach is focusing on outcomes

- Use the results of the Invisibility Index Tool as a baseline for your feelings. Complete the questionnaire on a frequent basis. The expected fluctuation that will occur helps you to see what normal looks like as you try to figure out why your answers might have changed over time.

In the end, that which can be detected can be treated. When the roots on our tree are poisoned, the leaves will inevitably fall off. Then it will be too late to do anything about it. The secret is to try to control the disease before you need a cure. If you are able to do that, you can start on a course of treatment and not have to look frantically for a miracle to occur. Let's start on a path back to health and become ALIVE again.

Chapter Five

IT TAKES A VILLAGE TO CREATE A MASTERPIECE

*B*efore an artist takes out a canvas and selects the material they will use to create their masterpiece, they usually have a vision in their head of what they want to paint. The first thing the artist does is set up the easel upon which the canvas will rest. If even one leg of the easel is of unequal height, or not standing firm and steady, the creation process can't commence. The canvas will fall and the paint will splatter everywhere.

The process of engagement is similar. Without full participation from all three legs of the easel, the "work" will often end in disaster. To ensure that your work/life canvas is on solid footing, everyone must be an active and willing participant in creating the masterpiece. That doesn't mean all three parties have the same role; in fact they each have distinctly different ones. It's how the collective work comes together that results in achieving the mecca of high engagement.

Painting is an art that goes back to the beginning of time, with some of the world's greatest masterpieces created by solo artists (think Michelangelo, Picasso, etc.). However, in our work lives it usually takes more than one person to bring a company's vision to life; it really takes a collective village with everyone having a distinct yet important role.

PAINT BY THE NUMBERS

When I was a child, I was never very good at art projects. I remember my mom buying me a coloring book that had numbers on each page in different sections that correlated to a specific crayon. I couldn't go wrong. I had the formula to stay within the lines and choose the appropriate color. Thinking back to my corporate career, it was clear to me that for a long time I worked in environments that used an old school method of "painting a masterpiece."

Businesses have always strived for three equal legs to stand on when creating and executing their vision. That was the cornerstone for most of my corporate career: two legs of the easel were immediately delegated to the roles of manager and employee. The third leg was assigned to the human resources department, which many see as the link between the manager and the employee. Traditionally, HR took the lead in ensuring that they handled employee engagement on behalf of the CEO and their senior leadership team. While this was going on, the executives stayed stationary in the picture frame (usually behind closed doors in their top-floor offices), letting the artists do the painting for them.

While this metaphorical easel was balanced from the standpoint of having all three legs assigned to these particular handlers, it clearly was not and is not the right formula for creating a masterpiece. Looking back at the old school way of thinking, the responsibility for engagement was definitely not a balanced equation. Employees had very little accountability for their own level of commitment and satisfaction in the workplace. Depending on two factors, managers had a varying degree of responsibility. These included: 1) their own level of personal engagement in the workplace and 2) whether or not others held them accountable for attaining high levels of engagement in their own departments.

On the other hand, human resources professionals were quick to take ownership for engagement, falsely believing that it would give them a high degree of credibility if they lifted the burden from their already overworked managers. In truth, all they did was give the managers permission to pass on the responsibility for the critical role of engaging their people.

In today's new normal business environment, the old school methods that previously served generations so well just aren't cutting it. That's part of the reason why the number of people who identify themselves as disengaged at work is skyrocketing.

CONGRATULATIONS, YOU ARE NOW A CEO

The world of work has changed and the future of the workplace looks quite different from that of prior generations. When we were all kids, the sky was the limit when it came to our future aspirations. Each and every day, parents indulged the fantasies of their children who felt they were destined to become firemen, police officers, nurses, cowboys, ballerinas, the next great entrepreneur, or even president of the United States of America. Many people even dreamed of becoming the boss of a publicly owned company or their own startup. Now, few realistically believe that will actually happen.

But I have some exciting news for you. You don't need to be the boss or CEO to change the world. What if I told you that as of today you are promoted? And I am not talking about a small step up the ladder either. As of today, you are being promoted to the role of CEO. Sounds exciting, right? Your first response may be to question my sanity and wonder exactly what I'm smoking. The truth is I'm not talking about becoming a chief executive officer. Who would want that stress and pressure? **I'm talking about promoting you to become a Chief *Engagement* Officer.** This is a career goal that everyone must aspire to if we are to reverse the trend toward disengagement in today's society.

Engagement doesn't happen without ownership and hard work. It can't just fall on the shoulders of one person, but rather requires equal but different contributions from senior leaders, managers, and employees alike. That's how to create the magic of an engaged and committed workforce. Thus, chief engagement officers provide an undeniable boost to morale and the ability for the entire workforce to reconnect and reengage in a more meaningful manner of doing business.

You don't always need an easel holding a canvas to paint a picture in the updated school approach to management. You can do it via technology and other new wave methods. What hasn't changed is that it still takes three equal legs to support our painting. However, what's different is that the people holding up the painting have changed. While managers and employees still make up two-thirds of the support system, now the senior leaders (including the real CEO) have taken responsibility for the third leg, coming down from the frame (and from behind their closed doors) to be active participants in the quest for engagement. Each one individually cannot master engagement; it takes involvement from all three parties to create the masterpiece.

THE ROLE OF THE REAL CEO

Are you ready to exchange the widely accepted definition of a CEO for my new and exciting one? While executives commonly direct behavior and decisions, engagers relate and celebrate unique and individual thoughts. No matter how big or small the company, the key aspects required to create and sustain a culture of engagement are the same for the real CEO and their senior leadership team. Here are some of the most important keys for this group.

- **Understand and communicate the ROI of engagement.**
  There is *always* a positive return when companies invest in engaging their most important asset—their employees. As

we highlighted in chapter one, there are a slew of metrics that effectively capture the ROI of engagement. These can include an increase in profitability and shareholder values or even a reduction in turnover or an increase in customer satisfaction, for starters. The CEO should make sure he first understands the ROI and then convey the importance of it to everyone in the company.

- **Set clear roles and responsibilities for the leadership team.** The tone within the company should be set at the top by the CEO by holding leaders accountable for creating an engaging environment (and being willing to take action when it doesn't occur). Engagement should be part of any leader's lofty goals and expectations. It must be spelled out in the company's mission, vision, and values so it can be lived by this group as they "walk the talk" for others to see.

- **Provide a safe environment for people to take risks and challenge the status quo.** It will serve to create an environment where creativity and innovation can thrive if people are rewarded for taking risks and not punished for failure. Engaged organizations are open to change, and from that comes new opportunities. People are significantly more creative and work toward unique solutions when they know they will be protected and supported, even if they do not reach their initial goals.

- **Create a culture of transparency and trust.** Employees desperately want to trust the people for whom they work. Trust is the fabric that holds an organization together. Being transparent about the decisions made and providing context for the why behind them will help to create the trust all employee's desire. When something rips apart that trust (such as can happen with the announcement of layoffs or a merger), the engagement of their employees is sure to drop quickly.

- **Communicate, communicate, and then communicate again.** Sorry to dispel the myth, but there is no such thing as over-communication when it comes to engaging the hearts and minds of employees. It's time for senior leadership to come out from behind the closed doors on the executive floor and talk to their employees. The magic of engagement relies on alignment and context, and that starts with communication.

THE ROLE OF THE MANAGER

Managers play an enormously important role in the journey toward reaching full engagement. So much so that we will devote the next chapter entirely to them! In the meantime, here are some high-level thoughts on their role to get us thinking:

- **Managers are the catalyst for linking people to work.** People want and need to feel emotionally connected to their work and the workplace environment. Their direct manager is the conduit to making that tight connection. If the connection is frayed, the rope will break.

- **A good manager makes people feel valued.** How hard is it to show people that they are appreciated for the work they do? It doesn't take much to convey that they are valued through a word or gesture of thanks. A surefire technique to make someone feel less valued is to micromanage him or her.

- **Instill trust through transparency.** Similar to the role of the senior leadership team, line managers should uphold the company's commitment to transparency by being honest and forthright with their employees. You don't want to be the one to start the water cooler chatter by creating an environment of secrecy and closed-door conversations.

- **Give their employees the tools and processes they need to be effective in their jobs.** How many of us can remember starting a new job and not even having a computer or access to the company's systems on day one or two or three? I know I can. There is nothing worse than being expected to perform a task for which you have no training or tools to accomplish your goals.

- **Paint an exciting picture for the future of what could be and should be, regardless of what is.** Like an exciting journey, it all starts with a roadmap that may involve some detours along the way. But, regardless of the obstacles that present themselves, you should always have an ultimate goal in sight.

THE ROLE OF THE EMPLOYEE

The second leg of our metaphorical easel is the employee. Like the managers, this group is also so important to attaining high engagement that they merit their own chapter. Here are some initial thoughts on this topic:

- **Employees need to take personal accountability for their engagement at work.** Just sitting back and waiting and hoping for divine inspiration will not lead to engagement. It takes an effort from each and every employee to move the needle.

- **Employees need to identify the motivation triggers that matter most to them and help their manager to understand what they need.** No one knows what you need to be engaged better than you. Find your voice and speak up. Most managers are not mind readers.

- **Employees need to learn how to work well with their boss.** Management is not a one-way street; it requires participation from two people who both believe they have a stake in the outcome of the relationship.

- **Employees want to be part of something bigger than them: something for which they can be proud.** Finding meaning in your work is one of the major cornerstones to achieving the magic of engagement. If you believe in the work you are doing and the mission of the company, it is easy to engage with the work.

I WANT A THOUGHT PARTNER, NOT A PAIR OF HANDS

So now we are left with one leg of the easel. Who no longer has their name engraved on one leg of the easel but has a hand in the creation of the masterpiece of engagement? It's my friends in human resources. Contrary to a long-held and popular but out-dated belief, HR does not (and should not) own the responsibility for employee engagement. That would be a big mistake because the direct manager needs to be actively involved in the engagement of his or her own employees. On too many occasions, I have seen managers pass off the responsibility for creating a culture of engagement to their HR partners, washing their hands of the hard work it takes to do this right. The result is that HR becomes a pair of hands doing tasks (think outdated action planning) that companies naively believe will increase engagement.

Human resources should be actively involved as a thought partner as the leadership works through appropriate strategies and reactions to employees' needs. While HR personnel are usually the ones who facilitate the diagnostics that companies may use such as surveys, pulse checks, invisibility indexes, and focus groups, they don't own the results and follow-up. Taking on that role sends the wrong message to company leaders about their need to be active participants in the quest for high engagement.

CEO OF ALL I SEE AND DO

Now that you've been promoted to the role of a chief engagement officer, it doesn't just end when you leave the workplace. Truth be told, taking ownership for your own engagement can easily transition back home with you after the workday is done. You have the ability to affect the way you react with your friends and family. It's your choice to engage or not. How can you expect the people around you to be a part of your engagement process if they don't know what's going on with you?

While this promotion to a chief engagement officer doesn't come with a huge raise, a move to a corner office, or even a new business card, it does come with a huge responsibility not to settle for being unhappy and unfulfilled, at work and in life. Creating an environment where your company can thrive and grow into a fully engaged workforce calls for the time, energy, and effort of the entire team. Michael Jordan said, "Talent wins games, but teamwork and intelligence wins championships." Hiring a smart and qualified group of people will position you to win. But to truly reach great levels of success and engagement, it takes the dedication and relentless determination of all three legs of the easel. Only then will you and your company be positioned to create a true work of art.

Chapter Six

YOU CAN'T SPELL REENGAGEMENT WITHOUT *MANAGER*

Why are managers like accordions? Have you ever thought about how an accordion works? In order to make a sweet sound come out of that cumbersome instrument, both sides need to be embraced in perfect harmony. If you apply more pressure to one side than the other, you won't exactly hear sweet music. But if you play the instrument precisely as it was designed, the sound it produces will be beautiful. So what does this have to do with employee engagement?

Think about it this way. Engagement is like a two-sided instrument such as an accordion. The left keyboard stands for top management, handing down a mandate to produce more in a faster timeframe, all the while keeping resources flat or even reduced. The right keyboard stands for employees. They require more of management's time, energy, and support. Each side relies upon the other for sweet music to be made. And therein lies the lasting conundrum. How are managers supposed to keep both of these sides playing in harmony, creating in-tune music together resulting in increased productivity, higher customer satisfaction, and increased revenue?

Managers can't play a harmonious tune if even one person on their team is disengaged. It's like trying to play a song on a piano missing a key. In today's tough business environment, managers can't afford to have a team working for them that is not fully engaged. Even worse, if your manager is operating on a low battery, then how can you expect him to charge and reengage others?

Most disengagement is silent unless someone is actively disengaged and wants everyone around them to know it (and potentially harm the organization along the way). As we've talked about in prior chapters, there are many ways to spot the symptoms and diagnose the disease. Our goal should be to think prevention first, rather than having to get out the cardiac-arrest paddles when it might already be too late. How do we get ahead of the curve and limit the number of people who are choosing to "quit and stay" in their chairs? How do we make sure that everyone is alive and healthy in the workplace? How do we ensure that the accordion is played properly? I've got the cure.

THE ALIVE TREATMENT PLAN™

The core concept that drives the ALIVE treatment plan is that an exit interview shouldn't be the first time managers find out their employee is disengaged and unhappy in his role. Today, many people choose to stay right where they are, even after they have mentally checked out of their jobs. There couldn't be a more damaging practice for a company that wants to be successful and profitable. But through ALIVE, this behavior and the damage it causes can be cured. This five-step reengagement tool is very easy to implement and doesn't cost any money, just time.

START THE CONVERSATION

The foundation for the ALIVE plan is a 'stay conversation'. In a workplace setting, this is a two-way dialogue between a manager and an employee designed to discover what motivates and engages the employee or conversely what is causing their disengagement—all of which impacts their decision to stay or go. Companies can increase employee satisfaction and address any issues that might surface before they become serious and irreparable by conducting a stay conversation. The information gathered during a stay conversation should be used to increase or reinforce employee satisfaction or reengage someone who has already slipped into a state of disengagement.

Managers should get into the habit of conducting a stay conversation at least once but preferably twice a year. It's important to note that this is not a performance management discussion. It's also not the time to slap a label on someone as being engaged or disengaged. Instead, it's all about getting to know your employees better, which if done right can pay huge dividends down the road.

ONE SIZE DOES NOT FIT ALL

The stay conversation tool is highly effective, regardless of factors such as job, level, tenure, and location. But when it comes to engaging employees, one size absolutely does not fit all. This is the same notion that forms the basis for all the situational leadership theories out there.

Today's workforce is comprised of members of four different generations, which results in a number of challenges and opportunities for the organization as it relates to engagement. It's a kind of "vertical diversity" that companies must pay attention to. Each of these generations brings their own values, goals, and communication challenges into the workplace, and it's up to the manager to be able to respond to everyone's unique needs.

Employee engagement from a generational perspective is a two-way street. Not only must an organization adapt its traditional old school practices in order to thrive in a generationally diverse setting; but also their employees must be proactive in understanding their own needs and seek out opportunities to engage with the organization. In the end, attrition and engagement are most influenced by an employee's direct manager.

Let's break it down for each of the four main generations:

Veterans (born between 1922–1943). Also called Traditionalists or Matures, these employees are children of the Great Depression, which helped to shape their strong traditional views that include respect for authority, hard work, loyalty, and dedication. They are dedicated to helping their organization succeed and getting customers what they need. They are great team players and don't let others down.

What they need from their managers to be engaged:

- The personal touch; provide face-to-face contact
- Take advantage of their experience by doing a reverse mentoring program with younger, less experienced workers as a way to transfer knowledge
- Show you value their experience

Baby Boomers (born between 1943–1960). These employees grew up in a time of great growth and prosperity. They really value health, material wealth, and personal satisfaction. They are driven to succeed, thrive on challenges, are highly competitive, and build impressive careers.

What they need from their managers to be engaged:

- Offer flexible work arrangements
- Give them challenging work assignments and movement, even if it is lateral. It's all about opportunities to keep learning and maybe use their skills differently
- Phased retirement options

- Reverse mentoring can work for this group as well

Generation X (born between 1960–1980). Sometimes known as the MTV generation, this group is motivated by money, self-reliant, and wants balance in their lives. At work they value having an informal, fun workplace but still place a premium on continuous learning and development. They are tech savvy and comfortable with change and ambiguity.

What they need from their managers to be engaged:

- Let them work autonomously

- Give them frequent, timely, and specific feedback

- Find ways to tap into their adaptability

- Offer lots of work schedule options, including telecommuting

Millennials (born between 1980–2000). Previously referred to as Gen Y, this group only makes up about 15 percent of the workforce today but is expected to grow into the largest part of the workforce in the next twenty years. Small and mighty is how I describe them, since companies are paying huge attention to attracting and retaining this group. They are a confident, organized, resilient, and achievement-oriented group of people who thrive in a team environment.

What they need from their managers to be engaged:

- Foster an environment where differences are respected and valued and people are judged solely by their contributions

- Let them work with other bright, creative people in a collaborative environment

- Provide meaning for them by connecting their actions at work to their personal and career goals

- Find ways for them to solve problems and turn things around

- Make sure you are providing constant feedback

As you can see, there are major differences in what makes each generation tick. You need to understand and embrace the differences to create a culture of engagement. If you do nothing, the cost can be very high. Now, with the backdrop of generational differences at the front of our mind, let's take a look at the ALIVE treatment plan in action. Here are the five steps to keeping employees alive and thriving once again.

STEP ONE: A IS FOR "ASK"

It all starts with the "ask," or the first step in the plan. If you don't ask and listen, you are making some assumptions that are most likely incorrect. For some time now you may have suspected that something was going on with an employee and wondered if the issue was disengagement. On the other hand, you could have assumed, maybe even falsely, that they were highly engaged and committed to their job. You won't know for certain until you ask the right questions.

This all begins with a manager reaching out to his employees to invite them to meet informally. This can be done at a local coffee shop, a conference room, or the manager's office. It doesn't matter the location, but what is important is that it should be in an environment free of office distractions such as phones or computers. Put people at ease by letting them know this is a "touch base" to see how they are doing and isn't related to their performance.

Here are some sample stay conversation questions to get the dialogue going. I'd suggest you limit yourself to a maximum of six questions:

Sample Questions:

1. What is your biggest accomplishment in your time here so far?

2. What is the one thing you would change about your job, team, or the company if given the chance?

3. What talents, interests, or skills do you feel are most underutilized in this role and which you'd like to see used more?

4. What opportunities for development, beyond your current role, would you like?

5. What about your job makes you excited to get up in the morning and come in to work?

6. What about your job makes you sick at the thought of coming in to work?

7. What obstacles are in the way of you doing a better job?

8. What is your dream job?

9. What could I do to enhance your job satisfaction?

10. What would cause you to leave this organization?

11. What are your short- and long-term career goals?

STEP TWO: L IS FOR "LISTEN"

It is critical that the interviewer in the stay conversation pay close attention not just to what is being said but also to what is left unspoken. If the right atmosphere is created from the beginning— that of a conversation, not a performance discussion—then a two-way dialogue can occur naturally.

You should focus on the ease in which the answers flow during this conversation. Is someone talking from the heart or searching for what he believes to be the "right answer"? Someone who is engaged will be quick to speak up and share feedback, particularly if it can lead to an improved work environment. Even if someone is giving negative feedback, that doesn't mean they are disengaged. In fact, it may be just the opposite. Anyone going through the motions will answer the questions in as few words as possible and leave you without an opening to probe further. Awkward silences and lots of "ums" and "hums" usually indicate someone who isn't being entirely candid with you.

If you know how to spot them, your employee will offer you both verbal and nonverbal cues throughout the conversation. Here are some tips for listening effectively during the stay conversation:

- Demonstrate your desire to listen by taking notes, asking questions, and probing further on what you heard.

- Don't try to problem-solve in the moment but rather continue to listen and dig deeper.

- Listen for the hidden message, what your employee isn't saying that can give you important clues as to what really matters to them.

- Look for nonverbal clues that might say something other than what the employee is vocalizing (such as not looking you in the eyes if something is causing them discomfort or their face lighting up like a kid on Christmas morning if they are excited about something).

- Paraphrase back what you believe you heard to gain confirmation, and then summarize and talk about next steps.

STEP THREE: I IS FOR "IDENTIFY"

Once the stay conversation has occurred, managers should take a few days to digest the shared information. Based on that information, they will want to identify two to three concrete re-action steps they can commit to doing for the employee. These actions should be something that can reasonably be accomplished and are designed to reengage and reignite the passion of the employee. It is important that these steps tie directly back to what was heard and seen in the initial meeting.

These action steps don't have to be something major. They could be as simple as asking the employee to participate on a new project team or shadow a colleague to learn more about a different function they might have a long-term interest in or just committing to talking together on a more regular basis. One could also be a commitment to removing an obstacle that is bothering the employee, thereby making their job easier to do. The key to any step you take is that it should be designed with the employee's engagement in mind.

STEP FOUR: V IS FOR "VALIDATE"

The fourth step in the ALIVE treatment plan is for the manager and the employee to sit down again, preferably within the same week, and go over the re-action steps identified in step three. This process will serve as validation that the manager was indeed listening to his employee and that his recommendations are spot on when it comes to addressing the concerns or hopes shared by the employee in the stay conversation. This validation process is key to ensuring that the manager did correctly capture the essence of what's important to the employee and shows that he is committed to reengaging him.

STEP FIVE: E IS FOR "EXECUTE"

The final step in the ALIVE treatment plan is the simplest, yet the most critical. To paraphrase the classic tagline from Nike: JUST DO IT! This is all about following up on your commitments, executing your plan, and moving forward on helping employees to reengage. If you have committed to the identified action items and then don't follow through, irreparable harm will ensue and there will be no way to get this employee back from the despair of disengagement. In fact, it will create an even bigger chasm between the manager, the employee, and the company that will be almost impossible to close.

If done right, this treatment plan is quick, easy, and cost effective, with no lingering side effects. It's the best holistic medicine out there. I advocate for preventive medicine whenever possible and highly recommend that managers make a stay conversation a regular part of their routine—twice a year, and separate and apart from any regular performance review. This investment will pay off handsomely for a very long time to come.

People who have adopted the ALIVE treatment plan in their organizations have reveled in its simplicity and ease of use and report great success in reengaging people in the workplace. Setting aside a few hours twice a year to perform this preventive treatment can pay huge dividends. It's easy to measure the return on investment by utilizing the ALIVE plan. The ROI shows up by a spike in employee engagement, increased productivity, higher customer satisfaction, and increased profitability while at the same time reducing turnover.

STAYING ALIVE

The ALIVE treatment plan is an exciting opportunity to reconnect and build an environment where you're constantly taking the temperature of your team to ensure it is just right. Today there are so many stories of leaders who "get it" when it comes to engaging others. We don't always hear about them, however, because the noise of disengagement drowns out everything else. Here are just a few of my favorite stories of companies that get it right when it comes to treating their employees as valued partners. From my perspective, these companies embrace the ALIVE treatment plan concept on a very high level:

HealthEquity, the nation's oldest and largest dedicated health-savings trustee, based in Draper, Utah, truly understands the connection between work and home. As a company undergoing tremendous growth, their leaders realize the toll that long hours take on the loved ones of their employees. In 2013 they rented out the local IMAX theater and invited all of their employees to come and bring their family members to a showing of a popular movie. Everyone was given popcorn and drinks during the movie. After the movie, the party moved to the Costco store nearby which they had also taken over. Waiting for them there was a catered dinner and an announcement from the chairman that each employee was being given a $500 gift card to be used on anything in the store. One employee summed it up best when they told company managers that "what we love about you is that you care about our family." A year later HealthEquity is still seeing the ripple benefits of this event with higher engagement and a story that has now become legendary.

USAA, based in San Antonio, Texas, is a diversified financial services group of companies that believes having happy clients starts with having happy employees. Their employees work in the largest private office building in the United States on a former horse farm, where there is a plethora of amenities including a gym, a golf course, and tennis courts. USAA spends twice the industry average on training on an ongoing basis. Their employees are measured not on productivity but rather on their ability to resolve all the customer's issues on the first call, regardless of how long it takes. This delights customers and motivates employees. Managers empower their staff to use their judgment on all issues, including authorizing payments up to a certain amount on the spot. They use a unique team structure where team members can rely on each other, connect at an emotional level, and learn from each other.

Zingerman's is a gourmet food business group headquartered in Ann Arbor, Michigan. They started as a local deli and have expanded into nine related businesses. While not as well known as Zappos or Google or recognized for employee engagement, these folks are legendary in the Midwest, and their reputation as a great employer is spreading. Their CEO, Ari Weinzweig, wrote a bestselling book focused on his management principles designed to build a great business. He set out to build the best place to work by following his natural laws of business. Here are some of my favorites:

- You are more likely to get to greatness if you have an inspiring and strategically sound vision.

- If you don't create a great, rewarding place for people to work, they won't do great work.

- If you want the staff to give great service to your customers, you have to give great service to your staff.

- If you want your staff to give great performance, you have to give clear expectations and training tools.

- Great organizations are appreciative, and the people in them have more fun.

This is just a small sampling of the way great leaders and managers engage their employees. Here's what they have in common: they all understand that their employees will be loyal and work hard for them if they are included, feel appreciated, and are given the tools to do a great job. Does that mean each of them followed the ALIVE treatment plan? Maybe, maybe not. But what I am confident they did do was to implement strategies focused on valuing employees, listening to their team's needs and providing valuable feedback. These companies know that their employees have lives outside of the workplace, and they strive to make sure this isn't forgotten. And, most importantly, they get that it is okay to have fun at work.

PEOPLE DON'T LEAVE COMPANIES, THEY LEAVE BAD MANAGERS

Remember, ALIVE is a preventive measure for disengagement. It helps to prevent employee turnover and an unhappy workforce. But not every manager believes in these strong principles. In fact, for every good manager, I'd conservatively guess that there are at least seven bad ones. There is no science behind this number, but with 70 percent of the workforce identifying themselves as disengaged, that requires a lot of really bad managers. People don't leave companies; they leave bad managers.

Just as there are companies out there getting it right when it comes to high engagement, there are those organizations that really get it wrong. To protect the guilty, I won't call them out. Instead, to shine a light on what not to do, let's use the stories of real people who became disengaged because of a bad or ineffective manager:

NATALIE'S STORY

HE DOESN'T EVEN KNOW MY NAME

Natalie is one of those people whose smile just lights up a room. Her enthusiasm is infectious and she used to be a poster child for full engagement. She loved everything about her job and couldn't wait to get in every day. No task was too mundane or too big for her. Natalie was incredibly creative and not afraid to speak up and share her ideas. She was the connector in her circle, always getting her colleagues together for fun events. I saw her recently and there was no big smile, no energy, and a hint of sadness in her eyes. Of course I wanted to know what was wrong.

Natalie works for a company that underwent a large merger, which resulted in lots of organizational changes. Her group was now reporting to a new manager based thirty-five hundred miles away. He spent very little time with her group in person and left her alone most of the time.

Natalie would try hard to reach out to engage him in conversation, but he was always distracted and distant.

When time came for her annual performance review, Natalie was hoping to have a meaningful conversation with her boss about her work and goals for the future. Instead of a face-to-face meeting, she received her review in the mail. While reading it over she noticed that the name on the review was not hers but rather was that of her colleague in the next cubicle. Natalie went over to her coworker and told her about the review. She then pulled out a copy of her review and so did her colleague, and together they went through them line by line. All this manager did was take her colleague's review and cut and paste it into Natalie's form. Oops, I guess he should have changed the name. Not surprising, Natalie is now looking for a new opportunity with a boss who knows her name.

Here's a story that highlights one of the biggest underlying causes of disengagement:

SUSIE'S STORY

JUSTICE WAS SERVED

Susie took a summer job working for a high-end restaurant greeting and seating guests. Her first week was great and she was looking forward to a fun summer. Everything changed that second week when a new manager was hired who was young, crude, and a bully on a power trip.

If Susie had a minor slip-up, as everyone is prone to once in a while, this boss loved to pick on her. One day he had the audacity to snoop through Susie's purse and found her bottle of Adderall medication, which she took to help control her ADD and concentrate better at work. As someone who never used her disability as a crutch and has been successful both at school and work without ever having to expose her ADD, this was devastating.

Once the boss discovered her medication, he humiliated Susie at every turn and would even bring it up in front of other employees by saying things like, "You might need to write that down for Susie; she doesn't seem to understand things like we do" or "Did you take your medicine today? I'm requiring you to take it now to work here."

Susie began to get agitated and knew in her heart that this situation wasn't right. She wasn't comfortable snitching but knew that the bullying had caused her to become disengaged on the job. Most importantly, it just wasn't appropriate workplace behavior. She finally decided to set up a meeting with the owner of the restaurant and told him her story. To her surprise, other coworkers had also gone to him with similar complaints and identified Susie as a target of bullying by the manager. Two days later her boss was fired and she went on to complete her summer job as an engaged employee, feeling proud of herself for stopping a bully and turning a bad situation around.

So what do these stories tell us? It's that engagement of employees can change on a dime based on the actions of clueless managers who either don't know or don't care about the impact of their actions. It all starts with awareness, both of how you come across as a manager and also what the triggers are, positive and negative, for each and every one of the people you may manage.

Remember the example of the accordion. To create a fully engaged workforce, the left side (managers) and the right side (employees) have to be working together harmoniously and moving toward a common and collective goal. The manager has great responsibility for engagement and his own list of responsibilities to make the workforce come alive, but he can't do it alone.

To create beautiful music, everyone has to hit the same note. And with that in mind: employees, it's your turn next.

Chapter Seven

YOUR PERSONAL CALL TO ACTION

HELP, I'VE FALLEN AND I CAN'T GET UP

*H*ave you ever thought about what disengagement actually feels like? To many people it feels like being stuck in a pit of quicksand, unable to breathe or establish firm footing and escape. Even though you are a CEO (remember, that's every one of us), it doesn't mean the choking nature of disengagement can't swallow you up. The ground doesn't care who you are when it gives way under your feet. Regardless of what role you play in your daily life (at work or home) disengagement can ensnare you in its trap.

People mired in quicksand usually panic and thrash around wildly, trying to find a way out. They move their arms and legs to get unstuck and reach safety, but that only makes the predicament worse as the sand shifts and envelops their panicking body. The reality is this: to find your way out of the quicksand, you have to stop moving, remain calm, and cry out for help. Unfortunately, many times there is no one around to hear your cries and help to pull you out. That's because most times those around you don't know that you are sinking into this bottomless pit in the first place. Just like the quicksand, disengagement can be a solitary process— you endure it alone. Disengaged employees don't call out, but rather they silently suffer until they are swallowed up in the worst way.

If you fall into this trap and find yourself sinking into the muck and mire of daily life, it can feel like a safe landing is nowhere to be found. There's no branch to hang onto or a rope to use to climb out of the hole. In a real pit of quicksand there's no time to create an escape plan because it comes upon you suddenly and without warning. And that is where the problem with disengagement differs. Disengagement is not an immediate quandary. There are warning signs if you are willing to open your eyes.

THE FACE IN THE MIRROR

There comes a time when everyone should stop and really look in the mirror, not just to comb your hair or put on makeup, but to take stock of what's going on inside your soul and consider if you are about to step into an unmanageable scenario. Think of the self-assessment Invisibility Index Tool we talked about in chapter four as the mirror. Honestly answering those twenty questions by looking inward will help to paint a picture of engagement.

The first step to reengagement is finally admitting you're disengaged. As with any issue you face in life, it is far easier to come up with the solution if you can recognize the problem. Fear of the unknown is a paralyzing conundrum that can sink you further into the quicksand. But facing your truth may be the key to finding the escape hatch.

If you can't get a clear picture of engagement by looking in the mirror, find someone you trust to be that mirror for you. Give them permission to tell you what they see in your words and actions that paints a realistic portrait of your feelings about work and life.

THE VALUE OF A SAFE LANDING

There are examples all around us of ways that we are assured of a safe landing. As you near your destination when flying on a plane, you subconsciously listen for the grinding noise that signifies the lowering of the wheels in anticipation of landing. While there might be a slight jolt upon touching down, it's a welcome feeling. When a boat is attempting to dock safely, there are usually bumpers lining the pier to guide the captain into a tight space without scraping the sides and causing damage and potential injury.

Similarly, employees need to find their own way to ensure a soft landing spot in the workplace.

Engagement is like the wheels helping you to touch down in a safe place. It could even be the parachute guiding you to safety once you jump out of the plane. If you don't have a working ripcord to pull in time, your chute won't open. Everyone in the workforce today needs to have a thought-out plan for his or her own career. No one else can wear their metaphorical parachute for them.

I recently met with a very savvy female executive who told me about her own bout with disengagement. She struggles with the fact that the more she moves up in her company, the further away she gets from what she loves, which is the real tactical work and validation that come from doing a good job with the task at hand. She misses the creative process of hands-on work and doesn't get the same satisfaction from managing others who are doing what she wants to be involved in.

During the course of our discussion she explained to me that employees always have three choices at work. They are:

- *Be comfortable with the status quo* by accepting that this job may not be fulfilling and engaging, but you are making an active choice to be okay with that.

- *Find your voice* by speaking up and being proactive about your concerns. Don't be afraid to talk to your manager or others at work about your vision for what could possibly reengage you.

- *Make a decision to exit the organization* if you realize that it will never get better, and search for a more engaging situation.

She offers some powerful lessons in recognizing and understanding where her engagement pivot-points reside and sticking to her guns to ensure that she doesn't suddenly find herself in a quicksand scenario.

It's important for all of us to remember that careers are a very long and arduous journey. There will be detours and bends in the road along the way. It's not always going to be a straight climb to the summit. You may need to take a few different routes and even stop to look out at the landscape while on the trip. It's all about creating a palette of various skills and experiences that may have you moving laterally rather than vertically. One needs to be engaged in the journey, not blinded by the destination.

THE CURE FOR WHAT'S AILING YOU AT WORK

In chapter five we touched upon some key tips that every employee should do to ensure their own engagement. Let's dive deeper into each of them now.

Employees need to take personal accountability for their engagement at work.

No one else is going to take this on. All managers, if they are doing their job effectively, will do all they can to ensure you are engaged at work. This doesn't mean they own your engagement. Ultimately it is up to you. They can come up with ideas designed to reengage you, but it isn't a one-way street. Each employee needs to be a willing participant in the engagement process for it to truly be successful. Employees should decide if they are going to get into the driver's seat or just be content to let others chauffeur them around.

Employees need to identify the motivation triggers that matter most to them and help their manager to understand what they need.

Most of us aren't mind readers, and it's not something we can realistically expect of our managers. One of the most important things any employee can do is to be clear, in their own minds first, about what matters most to them in the workplace. Is it to do meaningful work? Is it to make a lot of money? Is it to work with a collaborative team on an important project? Is it to get recognized publicly for a job well done? There are a significant number of tools that companies use to determine things like core strengths, working styles, and compatibility with others, but these don't always assess individual motivators. This is something that is essential to who you are and how you work.

Employees need to learn how to work well with their boss.

Working together to meet a goal is significantly less taxing than fighting each other along the way. The best way to do this is to be clear up front on what's important to you in a working relationship. Anytime is a good time to have that conversation with your boss. In fact, most bosses will probably welcome this discussion. A basic foundation of leadership is that it should be situationally based on what each person needs from their manager at a defined point in time.

The best known and most widely used tool in the workplace is Ken Blanchard and Paul Hersey's Situational Leadership model. The foundation of their leadership theory is that there is no single best style of leadership all the time. Rather, the theory is based on the concept that leadership style is situational—based on the task at hand and the employee's maturity and readiness to do the job. Don't expect your boss to be a mind reader; help them to figure out what you need at defined points in time. Remember that it is your journey, and the ownership of it falls directly on your shoulders.

ALONE WITH MY THOUGHTS

Some words that disengaged people use to describe how they feel are "isolated" and "marginalized." Many times the isolation is self-imposed, but that doesn't make the feeling any less concerning. In this case it's a self-fulfilling prophecy because the disengaged employee, whether consciously or not, tends to shut themselves off from others by standing or sitting alone with arms folded—sending off a vibe that says keep away from me. Many times they don't even know they are doing this unless someone says something about it. While this next story happened to one particular person, it will surely resonate for thousands of others.

ROB'S STORY

WEARING MY OVERCOAT INDOORS

Do you ever walk into a room full of people and feel completely invisible? That's how Rob felt for most of his time as a senior executive of a major company. He'd enter a room where his peers and boss were gathered, either for a business meeting or a social event, and immediately feel like no one saw him. He'd walk up to a small group of people, and even though he knew that he said hello to them, he couldn't hear the words actually come out of his mouth. He would wait for someone to respond back; all he heard were the sounds of uncomfortable silence.

Whenever Rob made a comment during meetings, no one would respond to his words. They would either completely ignore them or move quickly on to something else. He'd go home and say to his wife, "I'm so frustrated. I feel like I just don't have a seat at the table with the other executives. Why is this happening to me?" He thought to himself, Am I to blame? Am I not competent in the work I do, or is it just the way things are around here?

One day he finally stopped listening to the silence and confronted the issue head-on. He decided to do a 360-degree feedback instrument to get some insights into what was going on and how others saw him at work. What he learned was that the majority of people perceived him as sad and unhappy in his current role. He was wearing his disengagement like an overcoat—one he couldn't see that he wore all day, every day.

Rob was able to change his own behavior once he had the insights gained from the feedback, which ultimately had a positive effect on others around him. First he had to recognize and accept that his boss had no desire to create a cohesive team, preferring instead to deal with each person individually. The refrain in his head changed from "I don't have a seat at the table" to "There isn't a table for any of us to sit at to begin with." He eventually accepted this notion.

Now that Rob was able to look in the mirror and see himself as others did, he was able to reengage by simply accepting what the environment and culture was like at this job and learning not to take it so personally. Suddenly his voice came back, loud and strong, as he pulled out the chair and sat down at a different but lively and engaging table.

YOU HAVE THE POWER

If you think others are marginalizing you, it's probably because you are allowing them to do so. There's a famous line in one of my favorite movies, *Dirty Dancing*, where Patrick Swayze's character says of Jennifer Grey's character, "Nobody puts Baby in a corner." There would be a lot more happiness in work and life if all of us who have experienced disengagement simply stood up and refused to be placed in the proverbial corner. Hating your job is the cornerstone of a miserable life, so why would you ever want to live like that?

Earlier in this chapter we talked about key steps employees can take to treat their own disengagement. Let's now touch upon some important **don'ts** that are sure to keep you in the quicksand of disengagement if you continue these destructive behaviors.

- *Don't* hang out and talk with others who are constantly putting down the company. Misery loves company. But in this case all it will do is cause you even more unhappiness and dissatisfaction with the workplace. Disengagement is contagious and spreads uncontrollably like an undetected virus.

- *Don't* fail to take responsibility for your own career; it's much easier to sit back and complain that you are stuck in a rut. No one will ever care about your professional and personal development in the same way that you do. You are the only one to gain from continual growth.

- *Don't* stay in a job proven to be unchallenging and unrewarding. If you do this for too long you will become numb to the pain that comes with being stuck in place.

- *Don't* continue to work for a bad or toxic manager. He will not magically wake up one day and turn into a kind and supportive boss. If you are a target of bullying or other abusive behavior at work, you will not come out a winner at this game. In fact, there are only losers.

- *Don't* work for a company whose business practices you can't support. Integrity, ethical practices, and trustworthiness are the foundation of a good culture that fosters high engagement. Not having these is a breeding ground for disengagement.

GET RID OF THE VICTIM MENTALITY

Many times we hear people say they've been victims of bullying in the workplace and that this behavior is what led them to be disengaged. I'm guilty of saying it myself in the past. That changed for me when someone called me out on it and said that I let it happen. Truthfully, maybe I did at some point. But I was clearly a target of bullying, not a victim. Being a target means that someone purposefully set about to create pain for you in the workplace (or the school, the playground, the bus, etc.), without you doing anything to bring it on. Giving in to this behavior and taking on the role of victim has led many a person to shut down and swim in a sea of disengagement rather than fighting back.

The following story illustrates how one person decided not to be a victim any longer.

JUDY'S STORY

YOU CAN'T FREEZE ME OUT

Judy is no shrinking violet; she is a tough, hard-charging executive who when provoked had a mouth like a truck driver. Most of her career was spent in the technology arena, but eventually she took on a career-stretching role to run HR for the entire company. While small in physical stature, she wasn't afraid to go up against the toughest executives to ensure that the workplace was free of ineffectual and inappropriate leadership behavior.

The chief executive officer that Judy reported to used to keep his office as cold as a meat locker. Even if she wore a sweater to his office, it was still so cold that she would visibly tremble as soon as she walked in. One day she decided to call him out on it and asked point blank why he kept the office so cold. His response was, "It's the only way I can make you shake in front of me."

This CEO always treated women differently than men. With his male direct reports, he created a "good old boys network." But he clearly kept his distance by not proactively communicating with the women who reported to him. He did not entertain any personal conversations and withheld information. When Judy confronted her boss about his cold and callous comment he told her not to take it personally. As the truck driver side of her brain thought of every colorful way to tell him off, the HR realist side knew it was best to be quiet and leave the office at the end of the meeting.

Working in this kind of disengaging environment led Judy to feel demeaned, marginalized, and unnecessary. She felt herself sinking into the quicksand and knew that something had to change, and fast, if she was to get out of the pit. For Judy, the right answer was to follow her long-held dream to start her own company. She worked hard to get everything lined up to be able to make this move, and the day came when she was able to tell the CEO she was retiring. While I don't know for certain, I hope she walked in wearing a fur coat, gloves, and a scarf to ward off the chill along with a very large (and warm) grin on her face.

THE POWER OF AN "I-MESSAGE"

With bosses or colleagues or clients, staying silent can only serve to create a big helping of frustration and anger when things are not going right at work. That's a sure recipe for disengagement. However, the worst thing someone can do is to let it all build up till it explodes in a confrontational moment that can't be stuffed back in the bottle.

Confrontation only makes the problem bigger than it actually is and can create a fracture in a relationship that is hard to repair. So what can you do if you want to get your feelings out to the other person? That's where the concept of the I-Message comes in.

An I-Message is a very powerful and effective tool if correctly executed. It's all about thinking through the message you want to send and taking the anger and confrontational tone out by turning it around so your feelings lead the dialogue. For example, if you are unhappy with a comment someone made to you, such as telling you that you did a bad job, the worst thing you can say is "You had no right to tell me that I did a bad job."

With a less confrontational I-Message tone, the same thing would sound something like this: "I wanted to let you know how I felt when you told me that I did a bad job on the newsletter project. I felt like I let you down, but truthfully I was dealing with some obstacles that were impossible to get around before our deadline. I followed up directly to let you know about my concerns but I never heard back so I just went with what I had."

When done correctly, I-Messages allow the sender to maintain a modicum of control in the conversation. It's also important not to raise your voice and to keep your tone light when speaking in order to be heard.

IF YOU DON'T ASK, YOU WON'T GET

While the main premise of the ALIVE treatment plan is that a manager should have regular stay conversations with his employee, that doesn't mean an employee can't make the first move. If you have a boss that isn't making an effort to connect with you, then you need to take the first step. There's nothing wrong with asking your manager out to coffee or for an in-office meeting. Don't put him on guard by being secretive about your reason for the meeting. Let him know that you want to connect and chat about how things are going. That takes away the fear that you are going to come in and resign or confront him about something negative. Just be upfront and honest and turn the tables, but in a good way.

You don't need to wait for your manager to ask you questions. Instead you can start out by letting him know that you like working for XYZ Company and look forward to building a successful career there. Now here's where you might say that the "but" is coming. It is, but it doesn't have to be done in a negative manner. Going back to the conversation about the I-Message, here's where you might say something like "I really like being the finance manager for the consumer products division, and my hope is to one day take these skills I'm learning and transition to a role as a product manager so I can have P&L responsibility and run a business group someday."

Now you have opened the door in a positive way, which can lead to a discussion about what your career aspirations are, what obstacles are in your way, and what can be done to engage you in the work to help you reach your ultimate goal. Take charge of the conversation and throw out some ideas for your manager to think about that would allow you to reengage in a mutually beneficial way.

There's nothing worse than leaving a company because you were disengaged and having someone you used to work with say after the fact, "Why didn't we know you felt that way?" and your response is, "Because no one asked me." Remember, disengagement is treatable!

DON'T WORRY, BE HAPPY

In the smash hit by Bobby McFerrin, which debuted in September 1988, he wrote the following words of wisdom:

> *Don't worry don't do it, be happy*
> *Put a smile on your face*
> *Don't bring everybody down like this*
> *Don't worry, it will soon pass*
> *Whatever it is*
> *Don't worry, be happy*

This could be the theme song for those afflicted by disengagement. You have a choice; it isn't something that is out of your control. Let's end this chapter by focusing on my personal top ten list of how to be happy at work:

1. **It's always your choice.** You are the only person who can make the choice for you to be happy at work. Even in the face of negative aspects of the workplace, you need to think positively. You can do this by looking for those things that are good, and not dwell only on the bad stuff. Stay away from negative people and associate with those who are happy at work; it will rub off on you.

2. **Take charge of your own development.** No one cares about your development more than you. Today's careers are all about moving from one role to another, gathering experiences for your portfolio along the way. Lateral moves and stretch assignments are more important than following a straight line up. Don't be afraid to raise your hand and ask for something more.

3. **Don't be shy—ask for feedback.** For most people, the annual performance review is the only time they get feedback, and it's the most anxiety-producing process around. Millennials and Gen Xers have turned this process on its head by asking their managers for constant feedback. They want to know, early and often, how they are doing. For some people it's the only time they get any acknowledgment of what they are doing well. For others it's the chance to fix something that might not be working as well before it becomes an insurmountable problem. Since we've already determined that each of us is responsible for our own development, getting feedback is a key part of the equation.

4. **Gather your support system.** Find a group of supportive people who share similar backgrounds, experiences, and lifestyles as you. This can help to take some of the pressure off you at work by having your "team" to whom you can safely voice your feelings.

5. **Don't try to change others.** You can't change anyone else, only the way you react to him or her. Don't let other people's

actions impact your journey. There will be colleagues that rub you the wrong way at some point, and if you let them get to you they will have control over your engagement at work.

6. **Avoid negativity.** Making the decision to be happy at work means avoiding gossip, negative conversations, and the unhappy people you can't change. No matter how positive you may be personally, negative people can have an impact on how you feel. They tend to suck up all the oxygen in the air, leaving you out of breath and frustrated.

7. **Keep personal problems out of the workplace.** When you are overwhelmed by personal problems, it's really hard to be happy and productive at work. Also, your colleagues don't want to drown in your problems, even if they seem interested. Trust me when I say they aren't!

8. **Focus on the positive.** Even though you may not love your job, there is always some aspect of it that you do like. Find that nugget and focus on it, along with ways to incorporate it into other aspects of your day.

9. **Make friends.** Most people laugh at the "Do you have a best friend at work?" question that is part of the Gallup Q12 employee engagement survey. But truthfully it is important. Given the number of hours we all spend on the job, it is important to have a small group of people you can really count on for support, resources, sharing, and caring.

10. **Have a "get out of jail" fund at the ready.** Sometimes you just need to leave a job; there is no other right answer. There is nothing worse than realizing this and not having the ability to do so because of money worries. It used to be both money and health insurance that tied you to a bad job, but now with the Affordable Care Act, you can get other insurance. However, there is no easy answer for the money question. You need to put aside resources that give you the freedom to walk away on your terms.

Remember, the power is in your hands. Disengagement isn't something that happens to you, it is something that you allow to happen.

We all have the personal responsibility to remain engaged. If not for us, then for our family, our friends, our business, and the consumers that rely on the companies for which we work. Without purpose, there is no engagement. With purpose, people feel more enlightened, excited, and propelled by a personal call of action that keeps them engaged and focused on building amazing results on both a personal and professional level.

Chapter Eight

REENGAGING WITH LIFE

*L*et's face it; disengagement has an unbelievable impact on the lives of us all. It may manifest itself as a small crack in the dam, but it can eventually cause the dam to break and open the floodgates to something monumental. It's like a small ripple in the ocean because of a light breeze that without warning gathers momentum and turns into gale-force winds. Left unchecked, it can cause a tidal wave and gain the power to create massive damage, destroying everything in its wake.

Most people don't wake up and think about whether or not they are going to be engaged (or disengaged) that particular day. It's a part of us, but it's not something we tend to slap a label on daily. Within our lives, our level of engagement is ingrained in all we do, but it's usually lurking under the surface just waiting for a reason to come to the forefront. It's like a frozen lake. That coat of ice may look strong and able to support your weight, but if it can't you will find yourself drowning in freezing cold water. Disengagement resides deep in your heart and soul and only truly plays a factor if your outer layer cannot support the pressure it ultimately places on your inner thoughts and feelings.

Once you allow disengagement into your life, it quickly alters the direction of your journey. This normally starts with issues you might have at work. But it eventually hides in your briefcase or pockets and sneaks into your home, personal life, and family. It can infect your home, your spouse, and your children. And at times the reverse occurs. It can develop due to issues at home and then carry over into the workplace. No matter how or where it starts, this is a disease that spreads without warning.

DEATH BY A THOUSAND PAPER CUTS

Disengagement isn't a one-time event. There may have been a thick layer of ice to protect you from the water below, but the safeguard eventually thaws and isn't so safe anymore. Each and every rise in the temperature makes the thick coat of ice more susceptible and less capable of supporting your weight. It's a culmination of many things that come together in a slow torturous manner. Each paper cut leaves a small scar that eventually hardens your soul. Your boss passed you over for a promotion in favor of someone less competent—paper cut. A project you spent months working on received no positive recognition—paper cut. Your spouse yelled at you because you came home tired and didn't help with the kids—paper cut.

It becomes more difficult to manage the damage as the bleeding comes from different areas. You don't have time to heal when all these cuts happen one after the other. When they do finally heal they leave an ugly scar behind as a reminder of your experiences. Disengagement acts as a big scar that forms over your heart as you try to find a way to deal with the pain and suffering.

IT'S TIME FOR A MIND SHIFT ABOUT MIND SHARE

There are many versions out there regarding the oft-used 80/20 rule. Generally speaking, these indicate that 80 percent of your outcomes derive from 20 percent of your inputs. However, let's put forth a new version of that rule that necessitates a mind shift we all need to make regarding finding harmony in the two competing sides of life: work and home.

To attain that harmony, spend no more than 20 percent of your time on personal issues at work. That can mean anything from thinking about things occurring at home, issues with which you are dealing, personal phone calls or emails, and the like. Once outside the workplace, you should spend no more than 20 percent of your time thinking about, or actually doing, office-related work. If you expend more time and energy than that, the two worlds begin to blur in a way that negatively impacts engagement, both at work and in life.

The result of implementing the 80/20 rule into your behavioral norms is...

TURNING A NEGATIVE INTO A POSITIVE

Work-life (or life-work as many now call it) is a dance that people do on a daily basis as they try to find the correct balance between these two facets of their existence. Many threads tie work and home together, but none are so strong as the connector called engagement. It is the fabric that truly ties it all together.

Once you arrive home from work, disengagement doesn't always have to show up in a negative way. The same concept goes for the reverse (from home to work). There are people who are disengaged at work who truly believe they are better partners and parents when they get home. They feel this way because they tend not to stay late at work, and when they get home they put away their computers and smart phones and don't check in or connect with the office. Even though they do this for a negative reason (their disengagement), it allows them to be more present at home. In fact, they literally reengage with the happy culture of their life after they leave work. But ultimately that can be a dangerous game to play. Remember, disengagement will inevitably swallow you up once the ice cracks.

On the other hand, if someone has experienced a traumatic event at home, such as the loss of a spouse or child, then many times they see the workplace as their sanctuary. It becomes a place to reconnect and engage with people who care about them. It allows them to replace their current situation at home with a productive opportunity to make a difference at work. Putting all their energy and passion into their work can be a welcome respite from the pain at home. Following the new 80/20 mind-share formula is a great way to start finding the right work-life balance.

MAKE YOUR HOME COME ALIVE AGAIN

The concept of ALIVE discussed in the previous two chapters can easily translate to your home life as well. It's all about being open to a conversation about what's going on in your heart and mind and the steps loved ones can take to help reengage you. The only transformation needed in the five-step process to take this from the office to the home is to modify the ASK questions. This simple adjustment can completely repackage this program so that it can be applied to the same problem at a different address. To reach this goal, here are some new questions that can help get the conversation started:

1. What are you most proud of when it comes to your personal life?

2. What are you most excited to do when you get home?

3. What are you most anxious to get away from when you leave for work in the morning?

4. What do you dread the most when you head home for the day?

5. When you look at your life five years down the road, what do you see?

6. What are your three biggest goals for your life?

7. If you could change one thing in your life what would it be?

From there, follow the other steps and really listen to the answers as you both work together to identify changes to create a happier and healthier personal life. The conversation can take place between you and your spouse or significant other, a parent and a child, or from friend to friend. Remember, the purpose is to connect and share your feelings. Keeping things bottled up will only frustrate and confuse you and your loved ones.

DAMAGE TO THE FOUNDATION OF YOUR HOUSE

As we've previously stated, what starts at work can creep into your home life without you even being aware that it has. It's similar to what happens if mold shows up in your home. It's invisible until you see a small spot, which can then quickly spread to other areas. What you may think is just an issue between you and your boss travels home with you at night without you even being aware it happened. You never made a conscious decision to carry it home, and you couldn't stop it even if you wanted to. Once the disengagement disease attaches itself to your body, no matter how small, it can spread like mold.

I urge you to isolate the problem quickly so that you can start working on the treatment and prevent the spread of the disease. It doesn't require a HAZMAT suit and a sealing off of all affected areas. What it does need is a willingness to act and not stay stuck in the doom and gloom of your feelings.

TOOLS AND TECHNIQUES FOR DEALING WITH DISENGAGEMENT AT HOME

Disengagement can cause powerful feelings of helplessness and despair that make you want to curl up in a ball and just shut out the rest of the world. It takes energy to deal with your inertia. There are things you can do to break out of this paralyzing state. So with that in mind, let's review the tools you've easily got at your disposal to reengage with life.

Exercise. Physical movement in its various forms can be a great healer. You can take a long walk and clear your head. Sign up for boxing lessons and let your aggression out on the punching bag, not your loved ones. Join friends for a friendly game of softball or basketball. Relax with a yoga class designed to reduce stress. All of these are great ways to physically fight the onset of the symptoms of disengagement.

Volunteer/Give Back. Helping others in need offers you so much more in return. There is nothing better than seeing how your actions can positively impact another. When you are in service to others, it takes you out of your own head as you focus on someone or something else. Look around you. So many great organizations can use your help. Do you know someone who suffers from a disease such as arthritis, heart and stroke problems, AIDS, or cancer? If you have a passion for helping children then look at UNICEF, Big Brothers/Big Sisters, or Make-A-Wish Foundation, among others. Want to save the world? Volunteer with any number of outstanding organizations that fit with your passions in life.

Counseling. Never be afraid to ask for help from others. Sometimes talking to a professional who can offer you an objective viewpoint is a great way to deal with the pain of disengagement.

Spirituality. Whatever your faith, seeking out a spiritual advisor to talk to can be a positive step. For many, their church or synagogue or mosque can be a welcome sanctuary from the stress going on in their lives. In this kind of setting you won't be judged but rather given a safe and confidential place to share your feelings.

Family and Friends. You want to bring people closer, not push them away when experiencing disengagement. It is actually one of the times when you need your support system the most. Let them in and open up about your feelings. If they know what you are experiencing, they can provide another safe haven for you. It's when you remain silent and alienate loved ones through your actions that you hurt your family the most.

Hobbies. Lose yourself in a hobby that you love. The happiness and fulfillment you feel when you do something you love can wipe away the suffocating feelings brought on by disengagement. You might even find that your hobby has the potential to create a moneymaking business down the road, providing you with an escape route from an unpleasant work environment.

Travel. Taking even a short trip can do wonders for your psyche. You don't need to go around the world to leave your pain behind. It doesn't need to be costly either; you can take a "staycation" right at home. If you've got vacation time coming to you, then use it. It is there as a benefit to recharge your batteries. So what's the point of leaving it on the table? You can even consider taking a "mental health day" once in a while where you do nothing at all or simply spend the day with your family or catch up on errands you have let fall by the wayside.

Take a Class. Continual learning can be nourishing to your soul. Sign up at your local college for a class on a subject that interests you. Take a cooking class or make pottery. Use the endless opportunities present online that can sweep you away to another world and open up your mind to new and exciting information. It's all about stretching your mind and getting out of your daily routine.

THE BENEFITS OF ENGAGEMENT

There are so many tangible benefits to being personally and professionally engaged. Work can be a source of relief and creativity. Engaged employees do indeed ignite growth. If you are passionate and happy about your life it will bring you good health and happiness and ultimately more success and wealth. With this at the front of your mind, why would you ever want to remain in a state of disengagement? What's the payoff?

I can answer that last question easily: there is no payoff. Nothing good can come from "quitting and staying" in your chair while on the job and bringing inertia and hopelessness home with you. If you feel disengaged, you need a plan to bring happiness and fulfill-ment back into your life.

ARCHITECTING YOUR PLAN

All too often people go through life without any kind of plan. They just put one foot in front of the other and don't think about what will happen if the ground crumbles from under their feet. When something happens to throw them off track, they tend to get para-lyzed and remain stuck in place. It makes much more sense to cre-ate a plan, long before you need it. Think of it as *RI*, or purchasing Reengagement Insurance. It's there as a "break when needed" pro-tection plan—just in case you want to call upon it.

Architecting this plan starts with you taking an easy first step to get going. From there the ideas will flow. I'd suggest starting with a very simple paper-and-pen exercise:

- Take out a clean sheet of paper and make two columns.

- On one side, list things that are causing you pain and sor-row, both at work and at home.

- On the other side, write down the corresponding action that could alleviate that pain.

- Next, review what you've got on the paper and prioritize the one or two things you believe would have the most impact on your level of engagement.

- The next step is to create another list: this time it's the tasks you will need to do to achieve your identified goal.

- If your priority is to get out from under a bad boss and find a new job, then some of your tasks might be to create an updated resume, look within your current company for a new opportunity, or start an external job search.

If your priority is to repair your broken marriage, then the tasks might include attending counseling with your spouse or finding more time for one another. Another great tip is to bring along a friend on the reengagement journey so that you've got someone to provide feedback and hold you accountable. While the first step is the toughest one to take, from there it gets much easier.

THE MOST IMPORTANT LESSON OF ALL

Throughout this book, I've had the opportunity to share some powerful stories about people's engagement journeys. I want to end with the most impactful one of all that pulls together the connection between work and home.

When writing this story I was reminded of a quote by the former heavyweight boxing champion Jack Dempsey, who said, "**A champion is someone who gets up when he can't.**" Now let's look at how Adrian got knocked down but refused to stay there.

ADRIAN'S STORY

I BELIEVE IN ME

If I had never met Adrian and just heard his story secondhand, I wouldn't have believed it. No one could have lived through what he has the last twelve months and still be standing, let alone thriving. I know what

I'm about to tell you is true because Adrian is my friend and I witnessed his reengagement and rebirth firsthand.

Over the last year, Adrian was living a lie, not consciously, but that really didn't matter. He was a square peg living in a round hole and wondering why nothing in his life felt right. At the start of the year he walked away from a company he helped build and run and quickly partnered up with someone he knew to create a competitor firm. From the start there were those niggling feelings one gets when something just isn't right, and within the year those quiet doubts became a roar. Adrian knows with certainty now that others didn't believe what he was selling because he didn't believe in the product himself. That realization ultimately led him to close the business.

On the personal front, Adrian struggled to come to grips with the end of a complicated relationship with the love of his life. He was also raising his son from a prior relationship that was fraught with complications. To make matters worse, he found himself in a very tough financial situation, which led him to go through a short sale on his home. He currently has only three months of financial resources left to live on.

Hearing this story, you are probably assuming that Adrian is scared to death. The reality is exactly the opposite. He took every body blow imaginable and has come back even stronger than before because he finally found the keys to his happiness. Adrian figured out that he needed to believe in himself first and then others would come along. He also took the time over this last year to dig even deeper in his relationship with his son. It wasn't just about playtime anymore; now it was about learning and getting to drive him to school and back. His heart shattered into a million brilliant pieces the day his son said to him on the drive home from school: "Daddy, remember when I told you I didn't want to go to kindergarten? I want to trash that thought because I'm learning so much." It was then that Adrian realized that his life was worth engaging in, and now he was able to be open to the possibilities.

With his rediscovered confidence and joy came great rewards. Adrian has gotten healthy, both emotionally and physically, and the creative juices came flowing back. He's now in the midst of working on an exciting new business venture that will revolutionize the industry in which he's involved. When I asked Adrian what the catalyst was for his reengagement he said, "I stopped listening to everyone else's voice, and I'm now just listening intently to my own."

THE CULMINATION OF THE JOURNEY

Disengagement doesn't happen overnight and reengagement won't occur that quickly either. It's all about accepting the truth that inside of you, something just isn't right, but knowing that it is indeed treatable. The key to successfully reengaging in work and in life is this: DON'T RUN AWAY FROM SOMETHING -- INSTEAD WALK TOWARD SOMETHING BETTER. Walking toward something means that you are being thoughtful and intentional rather than rash and impatient. Walking toward something means that you are taking back the power and believing in yourself rather than giving up and playing the role of victim.

If you believe in this mantra, then you can be healthier and happier in all aspects of your life because you have the control. No one else has the power to disengage and disrupt your life but you. Don't let anyone but you take the reins of responsibility for your engagement. **Tomorrow is the first day of the rest of your reengaged life and career!**

CPSIA information can be obtained at www.ICGtesting.com
Printed in the USA
BVOW08s1328050614

355473BV00003B/7/P